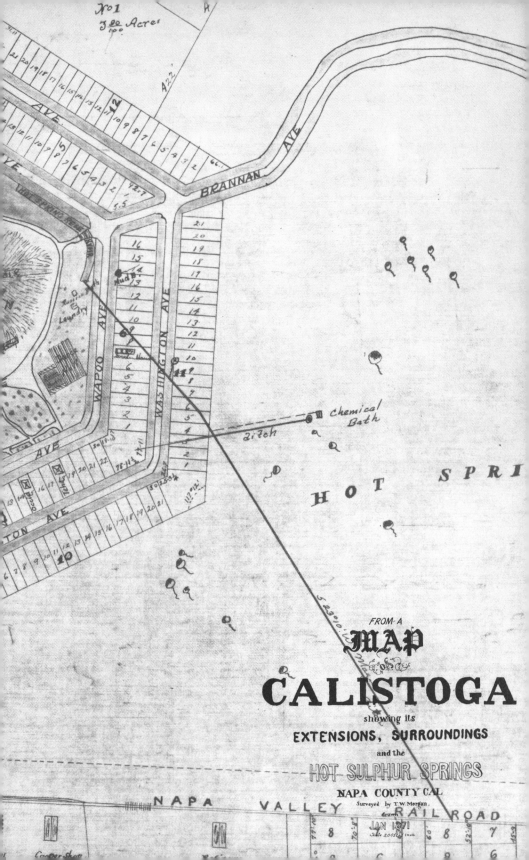

FROM A
MAP
of
CALISTOGA
showing its
EXTENSIONS, SURROUNDINGS
and the
HOT SULPHUR SPRINGS
NAPA COUNTY CAL
Surveyed by T.W. Morgan,
drawn
JAN 1871
Scale 200 feet 1 inch

The BRANNAN SAGA

Early Calistoga

by
Kay Archuleta

drawings by
Joe Seney

Illuminations Press
St. Helena, California

To the memory of my mother and father and to my brother, Tom Dowrick, who helped make this book possible.

ISBN 0-937088-02-1
Library of Congress
Catalog Card No. 77-79839

Third printing, 1982
Designed by Joe Seney
Published by
Illuminations Press
Post Office Box 126, St. Helena, California 94574

Foreword

SOME years back I wrote a story about Calistoga in its early days as a supplement for the centennial edition of *The Weekly Calistogan*, of which Lois Carroll Winston was then editor and publisher.

When Bernice and Ben Sharpsteen began work on their inspired project to reconstruct in miniature Sam Brannan's Hot Springs "empire", they also encouraged me to write an enlargement and updating of the original story.

Out of the renewed research, together with much interviewing and digging into old newspapers and books and family diaries and worn letters and clippings, has come this little volume. It is an attempt to bring together the varied comings and goings in this upvalley community from its Spanish exploration days, on through the heyday of that flamboyant promoter, Sam Brannan, and on into the early 1880s, when Calistoga had taken its place as a thriving country town surrounded by prosperous rural districts.

Mostly it has been a labor of love, though at times a frustrating one, especially when, after days and weeks of research and personal exploration and much questioning, there seemed to be little except a sheaf of undecipherable notes and unusable mishmash. Hopefully, there will be few discrepancies.

In this effort I have been inspired, too, and aided and abetted by Irene Haynes, writer-photographer, and by my family and friends, without whose constant prodding and encouragement this little book might have died aborning.

Incidentally, I was fortunate to know both Burt Adams and Elizabeth Wright, whose writings on early pioneers and settlers were a constant source of information, as well as Anne Roller Issler, whose books about Robert Louis Stevenson are known and loved worldwide. "Aunt Lib" was city librarian, and Burt had a little photography shop on Lincoln Avenue near the river. All three were very kind to a fledging writer, especially Mrs. Issler, who was here doing research on her own and who used to drop into *The Calistogan* office from time to time. They never tired of answering questions and telling lively and informative stories of this lovely and historic community.

Unforgettable was the merry twinkle in Burt Adams' eye and the equally merry whistle as he went about his work, accompanying himself between jobs on his ever-present autoharp.

In this effort I have also been immeasurably helped by Lelia Grace Crouch, her cousin, J. Milton Sherwood, and Thelma Tucker Tamagni, all of whom are descended from pioneer up-valley families; George Cropp, history "buff", especially about Knight's Valley; George Gauger, whose life spans two centuries; Ken Atkinson, Starr Baldwin, and Leonard McKay for technical advice and information; Earl Thollander, artist and author of "Back Roads" books, who introduced me to my right-hand man and book designer and illustrator, Joe Seney; Katherine Boyadjieff, Calistoga city librarian, and the staffs of Napa city and county libraries; Marion Bounsall, Marie Johnston Irvine and her brother, Robert Johnston, Pete Molinari, Fran Smigle, Joanne Zink, Mabel Petersen, Marcella Rice, Ella Spiers, Will Drew, Everett Fechter, Mabel and Oliver Mangis, Veronica Grube, Joseph, Golda and Richard Kettlewell, and many others for old photographs, family diaries and histories, maps, clippings and tips on where to go for information and materials.

And I am indebted to several friends with expertise in their special fields who have been so kind as to read over parts of this manuscript: the Sharpsteens, Sam Brannan; Lelia Crouch and Pete Molinari, pioneer days, the Indians, the mines and Chinese; Ellen Shaffer, curator of the Silverado Museum in St. Helena, Robert Louis Stevenson; Ella Rush Spiers, her father-in-law, Bill Spiers; and S.G. Rubinow, Dorothy Erskine, Milton Eisele, W.W. Lyman, and Jess Doud for overall historical data.

I am especially grateful to others who have written about Calistoga and its history and people. Since this is a book for reading rather than for reference, I have mentioned these sources in the course of the narrative, rather than relegate them to the conventional bibliography and notes. For other materials quoted I have tried to give due credit and sufficient references in the text.

To all of these and to many others I am humbly grateful; theirs is the credit for giving point and focus if this book succeeds in piquing further exploration and interest in the early days of this community. Without them and their constant encouragement this book would not have been possible.

Contents

Courtesy, Silverado Museum

The Beautiful Land

THIS is a story of the lovely mountain-girdled valley that lies at the foot of Mount St. Helena, from early recorded days to the beginning of the "modern" period of the 1880s. It is a story of the people and the land and what each has contributed to the other.

It is also a story of the Mormon soldier-of-fortune who poured thousands of dollars into the upper Napa Valley Springs Ground in an effort to make of it "the best spa in the world." His accidental naming of the Hot Springs Township itself makes such a good tale, so much in keeping with the make-up of the man who founded a town around the age-old Indian health resort that it probably really happened that way and so bears re-telling.

It was at a supper party one evening that Samuel Brannan of San Francisco, charismatic California pioneer, real-estate promoter and, more pertinent to our story, self-styled "father of Calistoga," was telling his friends, again, why he was pouring all that money, a fortune, into an admitted wilderness. After all, it was a long seventy miles from the civilization and amenities of San Francisco and reached only by horseback or carriage—that is, after one had managed to get as far as Vallejo in the first place.

Sam had intended to say, as he had so many times before, that he would make the place the equivalent, even the superior, of the famed Saratoga Hot Springs in New York. Instead, in his enthusiasm and helped along with goodly potions from his own distillery, he blurted out, "I will make this place the Calistoga of Sarafornia!"

Brannan stopped, and the crowd chuckled. But Sam was not exactly taken aback with the apparent blunder. Rather, the canny opportunist was not too much "in his cups" not to realize a good thing when he heard it. Delighted, he repeated the name. "Calistoga! Calistoga! THAT'S IT!", he exclaimed; and his friends were as delighted as he. The mistake became the fact, and Sam's "boom town" had been baptized.

1

Long before Sam Brannan christened his new town, Indians knew the Springs Ground as a great treasured health resort. They came from miles around to bathe in the steamy fumaroles and soothe away aches and pains with the volcanic mud and mineral waters, as had their forefathers before them. To the natives this was "Tu-la-ha-lu-si, the beautiful land"; and the hot, spongy turf was "Coo-lay-no-maock, the oven place," according to Miss Ivy Loeber, Napa County historian.

The Indian Hot Springs Ground was a health resort long before the white man came.

In 1823 a group of Spanish explorers, led by Don Francisco Castro and Franciscan friar Jose Altimira, had passed this way, looking for a suitable site for a second mission north of San Francisco, and found the Indians making good use of the strange potholes and bubbling mineral waters. Since it was their custom to bestow Christian names on everything they "discovered", they called the hot springs "Agua Caliente, hot water." However, they didn't stay here, deciding instead to site their new mission at Sonoma, which was nearer to San Rafael and encompassed a wider area for their missionizing.

It is generally believed that the Franciscan planted the first grape vines here, looking toward the production of sacramental wines. Altimira is best remembered, however, for another crop: the golden mustard which splashes orchards and vineyards in early spring, to be plowed under when mature, a valuable cover crop.

The padre had a burro which carried a sack of mustard seed with a small hole in the bottom. Wherever he went, the tiny seeds dropped to the ground. Altamira knew that, come spring, the party would be able to retrace its path by following the golden path of sprouting mustard.

ARLIEST recorded history tells of six Indian groups living in the Napa Valley. Spanish explorers knew them as "Guapos," meaning "brave, handsome ones." Whether this was their spelling of what they heard the Indians calling themselves is only conjecture which, however, does make a lot of sense. People of those days spelled—if they could write at all—the way a word sounded. And in Mexican-Spanish "gua-" sounds as "wa-". After all, it wasn't until 1843 that the G. and C. Merriam Company obtained from Noah Webster's heirs the rights to his "American Dictionary of the English Language;" and even if he were fortunate enough to own a copy of that rare publication, it isn't likely that an early explorer or pioneer would bother to carry a dictionary with him.

At any rate, "Wappo" was the term used by George de la Concepcion Yount when he came here in the early 1830s; but when Sam Brannan named the streets surrounding his new resort, he spelled the word "Wapoo." That's the way it is recorded on the official map made by Thomas W. Morgan when Brannan laid out the town. One may see it today, hanging on the wall of the city clerk's office on Washington Street.

When Yount first appeared on the scene, he estimated that about three to six thousand Indians lived in the valley.

The Wappo inhabited the area south of Clear Lake to the mouth of the Napa River. They were part of the Pomos, who in turn were the southern branch of the Yukais.

Indians living below the rugged range of mountains near the hot springs were called the Mayacmas. One finds other spellings of that name: Maacamas, Mayacamas and Mallacomes, the latter possibly being the Spanish spelling, because the letter "ll" is pronounced as "y." Neighbors to the south were the Callajomanas or Callaionanas, in what we now call St. Helena.

Incidentally, there was no Indian tribe known as "Diggers." Perhaps more in derogation than not, early Americans who saw the natives digging for edible roots and insects or making shelters in hillside caves gave them that name.

Tribal names were eventually given, in several cases, to the early Spanish land grants in Napa Valley. The most striking and controversial transition from the Indians' unwritten name

3

to the land-grant version is that of the Callajomanas. The early recorded spelling (March 14, 1841, to Dr. Edward F. Bale) was variously "Huilic Noma, Caligolman, and Colijolmanoc" and entered the history books in 1881 as "Cayne Humana" and "Carne Humana" when L. L. Palmer wrote his "History of Napa and Lake Counties." Anyone who has played the game of "Gossip" will have fun trying to figure out the etymology here, especially since the eventual spelling translates into "human flesh" and, of course, into controversy. Most historians agree that Napa Valley Indians, while warlike and good fighters when the occasion demanded, were not cannibals.

Erwin G. Gudde in his "California Place Names" gives a plausible explanation for the bizarre spelling: when he petitioned Mexican authorities for a grant to this area, Dr. Bale, "with a gruesome sense of humor, twisted" the Indian name "into Carne Humana." A more charitable reasoning would be that the good doctor only followed the prevailing custom of writing down a word the way it sounded. At any rate, the name "Carne Humana" was officially accepted in the records.

AN informative and entertaining story of those who lived in the upvalley is told by former city librarian Rachel Elizabeth Wright, whose mother was Lovina Graves, one of the child survivors of the ill-fated Donner Party. In "Early Upper Napa Valley" she writes that her father, John Cyrus, "saw the valley before man had made any changes in its condition."

"The Indians living here were largely nomadic, making their homes near waterways, shifting in small groups with the game and the seasons, leaving behind the ashes of their homes and their dead and often household and other artifacts." This accounts for the many Indian "mounds" found here, as well as the abundance of obsidian arrowheads, mortars and pestles and other articles.

"They lived on elk, grizzlies and deer. They pounded acorns and buckeye and baked them into cakes. They ate hazel and pine nuts, manzanita and madrone berries and edible roots of lilies and brodea, and steelhead and salmon, both fresh and smoked."

Depending on the weather, California Indians lived outdoors or in beehive dwellings called "wikiups" or in hillside caves.

The wikiup was a conical hut made of strong poles stuck in the ground in about a six-foot circle, bent and tied at the top, with a hole for smoke to escape and another at the bottom for entrance and egress. The wikiup was thatched with tules and brush and at times reinforced with mud. It could be burned when the village moved on.

About forty wikiups formed a village or rancheria (rancherillo), the Spanish name for the settlement.

Larger wikiups, about forty feet in diameter at the bottom, served as community centers, schools (for boys only), tribal meetings and ceremonies, sweat houses and crematoriums for their dead. Each village usually had two sweathouses, the Indian panacea for all ills seeming to have been a session here or at Coo-lay-no-maock, followed by a plunge into cold water.

It was this custom which unfortunately once made possible the slaughter of several hundred unarmed Indians near what is now Oakville. Although relations between early settlers and the natives were usually friendly, later on the Indians came to resent the white men who were encroaching on their way of life. More frequently than not, thefts of cattle and sheep were blamed on the natives, and many quarrels resulted.

5

One night, the story goes, a party of settlers, bound on revenge for what they thought were Indian depredations, surrounded the warriors in their sweathouse and killed them as they came out, one by one. Nearly the entire male population of that village perished.

When white settlers came here, there were three villages in the upvalley, according to Mrs. Wright. One was near Kilburn Creek below town, another on Cyrus Creek below Pioneer Cemetery, on what is now Rancho Calistoga, and the main settlement at Hazel and Myrtle below the city library.

The numerous shells found here, experts believe, were brought in by ocean Indians, who carried in fish and other sea products to trade for obsidian, a large deposit of which was in a quarry near what we call Glass Mountain, below town on the Silverado Trail. In fact, Indians came from all over, too, even as we do today, for the curative waters and mudbaths of Coo-la-no-maock, following the trail along the eastern rim of the valley, from the north over Mallacomes (their name for Mount St. Helena), and from the west along age-old routes. They also came to trade for cinnabar, to be used for vermilion war paint.

Many years later, other men would come here for that red ore but for another purpose and another use, as we shall see in another chapter.

The Forerunners: Yount and Bale

STRANGE as it may seem," says Palmer, "the first white man actually to settle in Napa County was an American. That was George C. Yount, hunter, trapper, friend of the Indians, and one of the two men most instrumental in opening up this area of northern California to settlement."

Originally from North Carolina, where he was born in 1794, he roamed and trapped the West from Yellowstone to New Mexico until he arrived in California about 1830.

One day, while hunting in what we now know as Lake County, Yount climbed by horseback to the highest peak of Mallacomes, to where the Mayacmas range splits into two branches, forming a "V." He had heard that somewhere to the west was Sonoma; but he was hardly ready for what lay before him, more than four-thousand feet below. The keen eyes swept the rugged scarf of the eastern rim, the rocky palisades and what many now believe to be the deep crater valley behind them. To his west and south lay another ridge. Between them stretched a long, fertile plain, a river meandering through its length, and smoke from many Indian fires rising in the still air. It all beckoned with a magic which was irresistible.

"In such a lovely place I would like to make my home!", he is said to have exclaimed, as has many a traveler after him.

It was about 1831; and Yount did just that, down in the center of that valley, near the present town of Yountville, named for him.

Yount found the Indians friendly, he reports, and he helped them as much as they helped him: he taught them to till the soil, to grow wheat and other crops, to sheer sheep and make woolen clothing. In turn, they introduced him to the art of dyeing wool and of smoking game and fish, and many other useful things.

Yount eventually became right-hand man to the mission padres at Sonoma and San Rafael, repairing buildings and generally overseeing the work of mission Indians; and to the californios, the Spanish settlers whose land grants encompassed huge sections of California. It was his association with Mariano Guadalupe Vallejo which happily led to his becoming a landowner, too. In fact, Yount made the first redwood shingles in California, for the home of General Vallejo at Petaluma-Sonoma, after a storm blew off the thatched roof. It was the general, whose land grant encompassed this area of the state, who helped Yount acquire, in 1836, 11,814 acres in the heart of Napa Valley, Rancho Caymus, which stretched from the present towns of Yountville to Rutherford.

George Yount first saw the valley from the crest of Mallacomes, Indian name for Mount St. Helena.

In those days the only way to obtain property was to be a californio—that is, to be a Spanish-Californian, or to marry into such a family. One also had to be or become a Catholic. Yount complied: he married a Mexican girl and also became a Catholic, though he turned in later years to the Anglican Church.

In 1843 he acquired a second land grant, La Jota, 4,454 acres on what is now Howell Mountain, whose forests supplied lumber for his sawmill.

Yount was the first farmer-rancher-orchardist-viticulturist in the valley. His home, "Sebastopol," became a mecca for immigrants from across the plains; and he invited more and more to come, including, in 1841, his friends, Charles Hopper and Joseph B. Chiles. In grateful memory, midvalley residents have since changed the name of his ranch to Yountville. His grave may be seen today in Yountville Cemetery.

AMERICANS were not the only newcomers to this area. Russian fur traders on the coast, at Fort Stweainski (Fort Ross), where they had been since 1812, had long known of the huge mountain to the east. Their Indians called it "Kan-a-mota", meaning "knoll" or "mountain," according to Miss Loeber.

In fact, an excursion party from the fort early in 1841 climbed the western slopes of that mountain, placed a tablet there memorializing the event and raised the Russian flag. That tablet was found in 1853 and taken to the Museum of California Pioneers in San Francisco. Unfortunately, it was destroyed in the earthquake and fire of 1906.

Gudde reports that in that excursion party was the Russian scientist and traveler J. G. Woznesenski. However, the historian disputes the legendary presence in the group of the Princess Helena de Gagarin, wife of Count Alexander Rotcheff, "governor-general of Siberia and all Russian colonies on the Pacific coast." Why, he asks, should the princess have braved the chaparral and the rattlesnakes?

The legend persists, however, that it was she who christened the mountain "Saint Helena" after her patron saint, Saint Helena, mother of Constantine the Great. Oddly enough, her name was the same as that bestowed on the valley sentinel by Padre Altimira in 1823, although other Spaniards called it "Cerro de los Mallacomes." Altimira is said to have declared that the mountain reminded him of the tomb in the abbey at Rheims, that of "Saint Helena on her bier!"

Etymologist Gudde prefers a third version, ascribing the naming to an American sea captain who laid claim to Fort Ross and lands left behind by the Russians. The seaman had also bought one of their ships, on the bow of which was the name "Saint Helena." At any rate, that is what he is said to have dubbed the faraway mountain, which is visible as far as seventy-five miles offshore.

The strange angle to this tale is that all three had the same idea, but none knew about the others.

"The Old Mill"

MORE important than Yount in the development of the upvalley was Dr. Edward Turner Bale, a young English physician who had served under General Vallejo in Monterey as surgeon-general of California forces. There he met and married a niece of the general's, thus becoming eligible for a land grant. Variously described as "bold, adventurous and headstrong" and always more or less in trouble because of his many debts and quarrels, Bale was yet well-educated and far-seeing, "a most spectacular character in the last decade of Mexican rule," according to Gudde.

In 1841 Dr. Bale, like Yount before him, petitioned Vallejo for a "land grant called by the Indians 'Calajomanas' or 'Kolijolmanok'." This was Rancho Carne Humana, whose development possibly had a greater influence in opening up Napa County to settlement than all the other land grants.

Beautiful Rancho Carne Humana encompassed all the upvalley from below St. Helena to the foothills on all sides, 17,962 acres, including what are now Calistoga and St. Helena townships: "two leagues of fertile land skirted on the east by wooded hills and overshadowed on the north by the purple crags of Mount St. Helena," wrote Robert Louis Stevenson when he came here on his honeymoon in 1880.

Bale commissioned the building of two mills—a sawmill near the present Charles Krug wine cellars and a grist mill to grind the corn and wheat of upvalley farmers, with a granary nearby.

Few of us have been so beautifully immortalized as has Dr. Bale. Of all the picturesque tourist meccas in Napa Valley, the "Old Mill" just off the main highway between Calistoga and St. Helena is probably the most famous. No other landmark in the area has been so photographed, lithographed, watercolored, oil-painted or wood-blocked as has this well-preserved mill.

Entrance is through a side door, opposite the former granary, now converted into a caretaker's home. A huge iron-grilled gate bars this entrance to unwelcome off-hour intruders, as do others at the front two entrances.

Two huge mill stones, imported from France by Dr. Bale, are on the main floor, one with the top removed to display its innards. Other smaller stones hang from various beams overhead, out of the way of souvenir hunters. A dumbwaiter type of lift to the rear of the mill buhrs once carried the grain from ground level to the top story, whence it poured down to the stones through chutes.

Prior to 1851, grain was threshed in the picturesque Spanish fashion: wild mustangs were driven at top speed around the enclosure in which the grain was piled until it was pulverized. The mass was then forked up until the wind had blown away the straw and chaff. Finally, after washing and drying, the grain was taken into the mill for grinding.

In 1871 W. W. Lyman Sr. acquired the mill and, in 1879, installed a turbine engine in the basement. The mill continued to operate until 1905.

In 1923 Mrs. Lyman Sr. gave "the Old Mill" to the Napa County Native Sons, who erected a stone marker and descriptive plate at the front of the property and opened it·to the public. In 1941 the Native Sons deeded it to the county, which, with its historical society, has restored much of the pioneer flavor and atmosphere. For many years Miss Loeber was its curator.

The big thirty-seven-foot overshot wheel, one of the few in the country, gives to the mill much of its artistic flavor. Water to turn it once poured from a long overhead flume fashioned from redwood logs cut in half resting on a high trestle which stretched back to the hill behind the mill to an acequia or canal which flowed from a mill pond fed by Mill Creek. When water was low, the wheel was helped along by a steam engine, added by Ralph Ellis in the 1860s.

This historic grist mill, known as the "Bale Mill," was erected by Dr. E. T. Bale, grantee Carne Humana Rancho, in 1846. The mill with surrounding land was deeded to the Native Sons of the Golden West by Mrs. W. W. Lyman. Restored through the efforts of the Native Sons parlors of Napa County, under the leadership of Grand President Bismarck Bruck, grandson of Dr. Bale, and by the Historic Landmarks Committee of the Native Sons of the Golden West. The restored mill was dedicated June 1, 1925.

Tablet placed by Historic Landmarks Committee, Native Sons of the Golden West.

The Pioneers

ENCOURAGED by Dr. Bale and Yount, American pioneers started settling on Bale's rancho in the mid-1840s, staying at either's homes until they could find their own places.

Among early travelers through the valley was Lieutenant John C. Fremont, who had come to California as an explorer-scout but who remained to lead an expedition against the Mexican fort at Sonoma and raise the American flag there. Fremont came from Marysville with a company of "revolutionaries," many of whom returned to this valley to join other Americans who were settling here.

Among these "first settlers" were names which have become synonymous with development of Napa Valley: John T. York, William and David Hudson, Benjamin, Andrew and Sam Kelsey, Nathan Coombs, Frank Bidwell, Henry Fowler, William Hargrave, William B. Elliott, W. B. Ide, Bartlett Vines, Peter Storm, who is credited with designing and helping make the Bear Flag in Calistoga, Nancy Kelsey, believed to be the first white woman to cross the plains, Colonel W. D. Ritchie, Robert Semple, Peter Teale, Ralph and Wells Kilburn, Elias Barnett, George Tucker, Benjamin Dewell, John Grigsby, Joseph B. Chiles, Charlie Hopper and C. C. Griffith.

HISTORIANS have a liking for recording "firsts", which have not always been in agreement one with another. Calistoga is no exception, of course. However, it is generally believed that the old Teale place a mile or so below town at Diamond Mountain Road and St. Helena Highway is the site of the oldest structure in northern Napa County. A home was started here in 1844 by Henry Fowler, who with William Hargrave, was later to acquire most of what is now the town of Calistoga. As was the custom in early days, newcomers stayed with other settlers until they could build their own homes. And so the cabin was occupied at various times by Andy Kelsey, who was to move on to Lake County to what is now Kelseyville;

Ralph and Wells Kilburn, who eventually settled homes nearby; John York, whose own cabin site at Main Street and Kortum Canyon Road is now State Historical Landmark No. 682; and Peter T. Teale, who was to settle here permanently with his family.

One of the Teale family, Reasin, better known as "Jeed", was a legend in his own time, according to Thelma Tamagni, a descendant of the pioneer Tucker family. "Jeed" was a familiar figure wherever he went, she says, because "a big white boar used to follow him, just like a dog."

The Kelsey hearthstone, which at one time was plainly visible to the right of the former Rockstroh home (Mrs. Rockstroh was a Teale) but is now covered with soil, was one of the California Registered Historical Landmarks granted in the Calistoga area during centennial celebrations here in 1959. Up on the hill above the home there is also a gravestone marking the grave of the infant daughter of Thomas Knight, first permanent settler in Knight's Valley, in the 1850s. On the stone is the following: "Sacred to the memory of Stella, daughter of Thomas Knight and Deserena, his wife. Died June 27, A.D. 1857. Age 1 year, 2 months, 12 days." Writing on the lower half of the stone is partially mutilated. Some years back vandals also threw the top obelisk to one side. Joanne Zink, who, until recently, lived on the property, believes the remains and possibly those of others buried here have been transferred to Pioneer Cemetery.

JOHN T. York came to the upvalley in 1845 and, by the stream which came down from what we now call Kortum Canyon, built the first permanent cabin in Calistoga proper, of redwood timbers cut at Dr. Bale's sawmill. Years later, when the Kortum family acquired the property, they built their home around this cabin. The structure was dismantled still later to help build the home and cabins above the service station.

The site of the York cabin itself was registered as California Historical Landmark No. 682 August 22, 1959, as a feature of Calistoga's centennial.

"Uncle Jack," as he was called by the settlers, did not stay very long, according to Mrs. Wright. Instead, he took his family to Sonoma, and, when he returned to the valley, settled on the lower half of the Bale grant below St. Helena.

Mrs. Wright goes on to say that "when Fowler and Hargrave bought all the upper part of the Bale grant in 1849, some 4,000 acres, Fowler made York's cabin his headquarters; and thus it became the nucleus from which grew the present town of Calistoga."

David Hudson built the second cabin here, across the road from York.

The new settlers wanted California to become part of the United States, so that they would be able to obtain land more easily. However, when the U.S. government offered to buy the land, the Mexican authorities refused to sell. Trouble developed between the californios, the Mexican government and American settlers. In 1844 the U.S. government sent soldiers and vessels to the troublesome Mexican province. There resulted the Bear Flag Rebellion. Its advocates finally gave up their idea of an independent republic, however, when they learned that the United States had declared war on Mexico May 13, 1846.

By 1846 more settlers had driven long wagon trains through the mountain passes to the west coast. Arriving in the valley were Enoch Cyrus and his three sons, Pleasant, John and Jesse; Reasin Tucker, Lewis Keseberg, William H. Nash, James Harbin and F. E. Kellogg. Kellogg made Bale Mill's iron work and built the house now lived in by the W. W. Lyman family. Jack Lyman tells me that this 15-room home is the oldest frame house extant in the upvalley, having been built in 1847.

Cyrus and his party had joined the Donner immigrants before the latter came to the Salt Lake area. The Cyrus group, fearful that a coming storm would delay them, tried to persuade the others to push on ahead but finally went on alone, reaching Sacramento just as the storm which caught their friends broke across the Sierra.

While she was city librarian, "Aunt Lib" (as Mrs. Wright was affectionately called) was guest speaker at Calistoga Civic Club's 1945 Pioneer Day observance. Her first-hand account of early settlers is a highly informative picture of the times:

"This group of families who came here in the 1840s were mostly from the Midwest. They were attracted to the Napa Valley partly because it was so lovely and livable, like a great unfenced park, its rich fields waist-high with wild oats and clover and golden with mustard, dotted with oaks and madrones and

15

peopled only by a few peaceable Indians and herds of elk and deer; and partly because this lovely domain was owned by Mexican land grant by two English-speaking men who were willing and glad to strengthen their own positions by giving or selling small holdings to Americans.

"Dr. Bale, who owned the head of the valley, further encouraged settlement by building a grist mill and a sawmill, paying the men who built and operated them for him with generous grants of land. So, by 1848, we had the following chain of permanent homes along the trail that is nobody knows how old: the Kellogg family, who built and were located at the old Mill; next the Tuckers, one of whose sons married into the Kellogg family; then William Nash at Nash Creek (what we now know as St. Michael's Villa); next the Henry Owsleys (the present Dooley place); then Kilburn, who had built and operated the Bale sawmill further down valley; Peter Teale, whose wife Mary was a Tucker; Fowler and Hargrave at the York cabin; and last the Cyruses, one mile above. Nash and Owsley were sons-in-law of Enoch Cyrus."

Elizabeth Wright, early Calistoga librarian and historian
Courtesy, Lelia Crouch

(Nash lived in a log cabin while constructing the two-story redwood house which still stands today. Its ornate neighbor, a three-story mansion, was erected in 1904 by Martin Holje, San Francisco glue manufacturer. Both homes are now the property of the Andre Boscs.)

"In addition, there were others who came and went, and the orphan children of the Graves family, who spent most of their time in the homes of hospitable pioneers. Two of these married and became permanent residents: Mrs. John Cyrus (Lovina Graves) and Mrs. William McDonnell (Ellen Graves)." McDonnell had driven a team across the plains with the Kellogg emigrant train.

Fourth-generation Cyruses still living on the original homesteads include Lelia Grace Crouch and J. Milton Sherwood; and Ellen's granddaughter, Florence McDonnell McCord, who still raises the same breed of sheep as her ancestors on the original holdings at the head of Knight's Valley. At the time of the first settlement there, nearest white neighbors to the north were at the Oregon line!

PIONEER women were as good shots as their husbands. The story is told of Mrs. Elliott's taking the children up into a "tree house" when William was away from their tent home. In the forks of the huge oak she would make the children's beds at night, while bears were marauding below! In the daytime she would shoot the bears from her tree perch.

Mrs. Wright recalls that bear meat, however, was not a staple diet, since deer and elk were tastier and more easily obtained. When the settlers added hogs to their barnyards, bears were hunted as a protection for their stock, says Mrs. Wright, "as well as for pleasure and profit out of the hides, and tallow was taken from the bears." Bear fat was a good substitute for lard. Too, "bears liked young piglets," and it became necessary to organize hunts to protect the hogs and cattle and sheep.

Mrs. Wright tells the story of "Old Hog Killer", a clever critter who regularly raided farms from one end of the upvalley to the other and always "made away with the bacon." Finally, all the hog owners in the valley, whether hunters or not, were called on to make an end of him.

"After a day of skirmishes and near-miss encounters with bears, the hunt took up the trail of the old boy himself and finally overtook him just beyond the watershed between the heads of two streams that drain these hills. He had taken shelter in a brush patch, but the heavy firing made it too hot for him.

"Below him was an open slope he must cross in order

17

to reach timber. To do this he employed a means of transportation I have never heard of elsewhere: in his frenzy, he encircled his head with his forepaws, curled up his hind legs, making a huge ball of himself, and rolled down that hill, over and over, like a great gray-brown ball." Nearly all of the hunters took at least one shot at the rolling mass en route.

At the foot of the hill he met the Cyrus dogs, who had meanwhile been following another bear up stream. They promptly turned to "Old Hog Killer" and soon put him up a tree, where he could be seen.

"Council was held on the hill above, as careful shooting was now required because of the baying and valuable dogs.

"Pleasant Cyrus, the dogs' owner, being admittedly the best shot, was helped up another tree, and the men below kept loading their rifles and handing them up to him, one by one. There Pleasant clung, shooting steadily at the brush-hidden mass of bear until either some one ball hit a vital spot or the many wounds had bled the bear to the point of death so he fell to the ground."

"Old Hog Killer's" hide, when it was stretched afterwards on the side of the Cyrus barn, proved to be the biggest ever taken in that community. It had twenty-eight bullet holes in it. That barn, incidentally, may be the one still standing across from the entrance to the Sherwood ranch on Foothill Blvd. At least, Milton Sherwood says his grandfather, John Cyrus, Jr., built that barn.

"Early Upper Napa Valley" also tells about the July 4 celebration in 1852. "People came from all over, including Captain Sutter himself. A whole beef was barbecued in a big pit, and one of the entertainment features was a fight between a bull and a bear in a stockade.

"The bull hadn't much fight in him," writes Mrs. Wright, "so after the bear had punished him enough to satisfy the blood lust of the crowd, the bear was shot and the bull driven out to nurse his wounds or die as best he could—rough times, rough pleasures."

CALISTOGA was a strong social community in its early years. There were quilting bees, horse-breaking contests, house - and barn raisings, and house parties. Entertainment included church socials (a good place to get acquainted, then as now!) and rare trips to Sonoma for a "big dance." The latter trips took several days, and the girls stayed with the hospitable mission women. Warm hospitality, dignity and courtesy were a way of life.

It was a typical social function which caused the death of several of the Cyrus family. A guest from the Moore ranch downvalley stayed overnight at the Cyrus place on the way to a wedding reception or "in fair" at the Elliotts'.

Unknown to the family, he had smallpox. Enoch and two sons contracted the disease and died. As was the custom in early days—there was no public cemetery until 1894—, they were buried in Cyrus family cemetery above Cyrus Creek, across from the present Sherwood ranch. A few years back, the family transferred the headstones of the three smallpox victims and Mrs. Cyrus to the family plot in Pioneer Cemetery.

That cemetery, sometimes referred to as the "smallpox cemetery," is typical of early burial places, some of which are to be found today in the upvalley. The stone wall and pipe railing marking the site are clearly visible above the Petrified Forest Road.

THE discovery of gold in 1848 didn't make much impression on early Calistogans, according to Mrs.

Wright, although, she says, many men lower downvalley did decamp for a while.

"Few valley people went into the mining camps, and few made money from the gold rush. They were neither gold diggers not mercantile-minded but homemakers, farmers, most of whom sold farms in the Middle West to come to the coast to get away from severe winters.

Besides being the site of the first grist and saw mills in this part of the state, Calistoga also had the first community church and school north of the bay—the White church and a brush shanty out in front of Bale Mill. Sarah Graves Fosdick, Mrs. Wright's aunt, was the teacher.

Understandably, pioneers and early settlers brought with them their great love of the land, which persists today. Agriculture has always been the mainstay of Napa County; and the family farm, orchard, vineyard and sawmill withstood the encroachment of larger commercial enterprises well into the twentieth century.

I. C. Adams, Napa Valley photographer and historian.

THE first white child born in Calistoga, December 24, 1849, was Sarah Owsley, daughter of Henry and Frances Owsley and aunt of Dottie Adams, the wife of Calistoga's recent well-known and loved historian Ira Clayton Adams, better known as Burt or I. C.

Adams, who came to Calistoga in 1882, has written what he calls a "sentimental early history" of the town, "Memoirs and Anecdotes of Early Days in Calistoga," a highly informative and readable book and one of the few sources of data about Calistoga in early times available. Dottie and Burt did much research for their account at the Bancroft Library on the University of California campus. With their permission, I have often dipped into the book for background material on frontier life here.

Owsley, a son-in-law of John Cyrus, was one of the town's first butchers. His neighbors to the north were the Kilburn brothers, who had obtained land from Dr. Bale in return for building the latter's sawmill. Wells Kilburn built a home at what is now Dunaweal and Ralph closer to town on the Teale place.

That line of pioneers' homes "along the trail that is nobody knows how old," as Mrs. Wright picturesquely says it, became the first street in the new upvalley community, Main Street. (In 1948 the town's Board of Trustees changed that name to Foothill Blvd.)

ANOTHER early settler, who had come with York and Hudson, was William B. Elliott, an aide to Fremont. One day, while exploring the wilderness beyond Knight's Valley, he came upon Indians caring for their sick in caves carved out of steaming hillsides and bathing in hot fumaroles. An arthritic, he persuaded the natives to give him a treatment. He evidently liked it because not long afterward he secured a 5,000-acre Spanish land grant from Jose Berryessa and started what later became known as The Geysers, a famous health resort. Today it is the site of a PG&E geothermal plant.

Elliott also built a grist mill in Franz Valley. Stones from this mill were later moved to Mark West's mill further along the stage route to Santa Rosa.

An Elliott son married Rachel Cyrus, but the marriage was an unhappy one, ending in divorce. Rachel then married a Heald, the family which was to found Healdsburg.

In 1857 Captain Frederick W. Franz obtained title to the valley which bears his name, with his mother-in-law, M. S. Silbert. One of his daughters, Minnie, married S. D. Clark; the other, Edith, married George Kettlewell.

The late George Kettlewell Jr., descendant of early settlers in Franz Valley, brought a copy of the deed to the area to the office of *The Calistogan* in 1957. (See Appendix 2.)

Publication of Kettlewell's deed and subsequent news stories and editorials in *The Calistogan* alerted the Calistoga community to the fact that there would soon be a one-hundred years' anniversary of its founding in 1859 and helped serve as a springboard for the 1959 centennial celebration.

Calvin Hall Holmes, whose family includes Oliver Wendell Holmes, purchased the farther end of the Berryessa tract in 1859. His daughter Kate married Calvin Foote; and her inheritance became the basis of the present Foote ranch. Florence B. Foote, granddaughter of pioneer Samuel W. Kellett and widow of Kate's first son, Calvin, now lives in town. The Kellett home was at Dunaweal, south of Calistoga.

Delia Parish Holmes, widow of the late William F. Holmes Jr., makes her home in Walnut Creek; and several of the Foote family are in the Bay Area.

Harrison Bidwell of Los Gatos and his sister, Annette Bidwell Hensgen of Middletown, are fifth-generation descendants of Alexander Valley pioneer Frank Bidwell. Their mother, wife of the late Stanley St. Clair Bidwell, was a Berryessa.

As more and more farms became established in the several rural areas around the town, district names became identified with those of pioneers who had settled there: Tucker District to the south of town; Franz and Knight's valleys to the west; Porter Creek and the Petrified Forest Road area to the southwest; Bennett District, including Myrtledale and Tubbs Lane areas to the north; and Kellogg at the head of Knight's Valley. Up until recently, Kellogg had its own store and post office at the foot of the Ida Clayton Toll Road.

Settlers and the Californios

ESPITE the increasing number of Americans coming into the valley, this area retained the warm hospitality, dignity, courtesy and easygoing way of life of the Mexican era. Understandably, of course, would-be mid-century settlers chafed under the strict rules for owning land which prevailed well into the 1860s. And so Americans welcomed and actively supported the Bear Flag Rebellion, which eventually led to California's being taken over by the United States as a territory. There were long court proceedings, usually decided in favor of the Spanish hacendados. (See land agent's document, Appendix I.)

But it was the Great Drought of 1863-65 which became a deciding factor and accomplished as much as anything to break up the ranchos. The rancheros had to sell their cattle, great portions of their herds, because there was no feed—this in a valley whose main agricultural product was grain.

At any rate, the easy-going californios finally gave up, immigrants gradually taking over the Spanish land grants. However, transition from the Mexican era to the death of Yount in 1865 was tumultuous. It was still much better for a newcomer to be "sponsored" by a californio who was a Mexican-citizen hacendado (landowner) when purchasing or trading for land, as did Sam Brannan, or just "squat" on it. Yount himself often said that the squatters gave him more trouble than the Indians and the grizzlies.

Burt Adams tells the story of the designing and making of the Bear Flag itself, reportedly in Calistoga. The story goes that the group of valley men joining Fremont met at the Grigsby ranch southeast of Yountville and accepted Peter Storm's home-made flag as the official emblem of their Bear Flag Rebellion, which was to free California from the domination of Mexico. The flag itself, says Adams, was fashioned from a design made by Storm at the Cyrus ranch, where he often stayed, and made up in four sections from the petticoats of Mrs. Ben Kelsey and perhaps others. The colors were red and white, each horizontal

Peter Storm and the first Bear Flag.

band being made up of two pieces. The bear and the star were the only decoration, the star, a blue one, being in the upper quarter right next to the staff. A picture of Storm holding his flag is included in Adams' book.

I T was one thing to acquire land; but keeping it, especially after the californios' hold on their grants came more in dispute, was sometimes a hassle.

In connection with a story I was doing for *The Calistogan* in 1962 on R. P. Tucker and the White Memorial Church, I received from Allen W. Welts, historian with the state Resources Agency, Division of Beaches and Parks, an article which well illustrated some of the problems settlers incurred trying to acquire title to their land.

The story had been written by state land agent Robert D. Adams and is part of the research made by him in the Bothe-Napa Valley State Park area. The park is a portion of the original Bale land grant which had been acquired by Tucker.

Tucker's right to the property, along with those of others who had received land from Dr. Bale, came into litigation before the U. S. government courts which were trying to settle the many disputed claims under Mexican land grants. Bale died before his ownership of the rancho had been confirmed; and his heirs, especially his widow, Maria Ignacio Soberanes de Bale, and daughter, who had married Louis Bruck, carried on the confirmation request through the courts.

Meanwhile, Tucker had quitclaimed a parcel of land for a church building and cemetery, the White Memorial Church, whose first pastor was the Reverend Asa White. Other settlers also became caught up in legal tangles, including Colonel Ritchie and Sam Brannan. The latter was buying up land for his proposed resort in Calistoga.

The suits dragged on for years through the various courts, eventually being resolved for the Bale heirs, but not before still others had become involved, including Dr. Charles Hitchcock and his famous daughter, Lillie Coit. Final court action wiped out the holdings of Tucker and the church. The church building was abandoned, but the cemetery still exists.

Hitchcock, who had bought a parcel of land from Mrs. Bruck, was involved over an issue of water rights in Ritchie Creek. Judgement was in Hitchcock's favor—a fact which became important some years later when Lillie Hitchcock Coit sold out to Mr. and Mrs. Ren Bothe. The Bothes in turn disposed of their property to the state, the area now known as Bothe-Napa Valley State Park.

(Adams' complete account of events leading up to and following the various entanglements of the Bale Rancho dispute is Appendix 1.)

ONG after the days of the Mexican rancheros and early settlers, the lush upvalley fields were still studded with oaks of all kinds and heavy with wild oats and the farmer's main agricultural product, grain, especially corn and wheat. Grist mills, such as Yount's and Bale's and Mark West's, were kept busy supplying demands for flour and feed for fowl and farm animals.

The familiar saying "wild oats as tall as a horse's withers" meant a year of good rainfall and therefore good crops.

Dairying has always been big in Napa County. In fact, it was Number One industry for years, along with its satellites, tanning of hides and skins and wool pulling, commencing in Mexican days.

The Napa Agricultural Society was founded in 1854; the Napa Viticultural Society not until 1881.

First dairy in Calistoga was that of the Ayer family, located about where the Louis Vermeil property is now, according to Burt Adams. Charles W. Ayer also built the two-story house on the north corner of Lincoln and Myrtle in 1875, which is still standing.

After Ayer, a man named Trufant ran the dairy. When William T. Gibbs bought the place, he built a processing plant to take care of all the prunes which were not dried by individual farmers on the familiar "prune trays", many of which are still in use today—for drying fruit and nuts and even serving as background for art exhibits!

Gibbs eventually leased ground out on Lake Street near Railroad Avenue and moved his drying plant there, familiarly known later as "Pruneville."

"Uncle Erwin" Kellogg and William Nash are credited with planting the first fruit trees here. Their orchards—walnuts, peaches, pears, oranges—and vineyards flourished along the Geyser Highway, the old name for the St. Helena-Calistoga Highway. Walnuts and olives more than one-hundred years old can be found all over the upvalley, still producing.

Old-timers tell me that not too many fruits did well here, however, with one exception—the prune, fifteen to twenty varieties of which were grown, with the French prune a wide favorite. The success of the prune was assured with the discovery of the Myrobalan root stock, a resistant variety, just as the St. George grape used as a resistant root stock saved the wine industry in later years, one rancher told me.

The tremendous popularity of the wine grape has gradually eliminated dairying as Number One industry in Napa County, and along with it the family prune and walnut orchard. But who will ever forget the lush green pastures with their black-and-white and red-and-white and fawn-colored cows? For years, before the vines took over the vast fields along the Silverado Trail, the loveliest sight in the valley was the Tamagni pasture with its lavish show of poppies and lupine every spring. And the beautiful billows of prune blossoms above the golden mustard and blue lupines once rivaled the spring glory of California's fabled desert flowers as a tourist attraction. The mustard still remains, fortunately; and, thanks to the wisdom of those who established the Agricultural Preserve, the extensive vineyards which have taken the place of pastures and orchards still command the admiration of a world of artists and wine-lovers alike with their inimitable display of spring green and amazing autumn color.

V INES took to our valley "like a duck to water," one viticulturist told me. Altimira and Yount planted the first, and Sam Brannan set out an estimated 100,000 vines. However, the wine grape was not extensively cultivated until George Belden Crane found that the Mission variety did well here. He was a physician and surgeon who came here from San Jose in 1857. An ardent economist, Dr. Crane spent many years trying to promote Napa County wine for the eastern market. He is largely credited with starting today's flourishing wine industry.

Another wine-grape pioneer was Henri Alphonse Pellet, who had charge of Dr. Crane's vineyard and cellar before building his own mid-valley. It is said Pellet imported about sixty varieties of grapes to test their suitability and adaptability to the soil and climate. The varieties he chose were for years followed by growers all over this area—reds: Zinfandel, Mataro, Grenache, Carignan, St. Micaire, Malbec; whites: the Rieslings, the Chasselas, and the Burger, grafted on what was called "native resistant stock". ("Pen Pictures of the Garden of the World, a History of   *27*

Northern California", published by Lewis Publishing Company of Chicago.).

The valley's main wine-producing area has always been from Yountville north to St. Helena, although many vineyards have continued to flourish in Calistoga from early days on. Lyman L. Palmer, historian for Slocum, Bowen & Company, publishers of the "History of Napa and Lake Counties" (1881), lists two Calistoga wine cellars as being important in the valley's wine picture: L. Kortum's "doing a very good business, on a small scale, having made in 1880 35,000 gallons of wine, which is pronounced by judges to be a first-class article;" and J. J. H. Medeau, "also is a small cellar, making only 12,000 gallons in 1880."

Kortum's winery was at the intersection of Main Street and Kortum Canyon Road. One of its two buildings, still in good condition, stands at the foot of the grade.

The oldest operating winery is Charles Krug in St. Helena. Krug was an assistant to Count Agostin Harazthy in Sonoma. He came here in 1852 and married Dr. Bale's daughter, Caroline, acquiring along with his wife a five-hundred-and-forty acre dowry. He planted wine grapes, making his first wine on a cider press, and built his cellar in 1861.

When phylloxera, the dread lice disease which destroys grape vines by attacking roots and causing leaves to wither and die, hit the valley in the late 1870s and early 1880s, Krug and other viticulturists were badly hurt. He died in 1892. Prior to his death, James Moffitt of San Francisco had acquired the Krug holdings.

When phylloxera hit, many farmers pulled out their vines and went back to growing grain and fruit trees. It wasn't until a resistant root stock, the St. George, was found in the early 1900s, that grapes once again came into their own.

WHILE Napa Valley is primarily agricultural, lumbering has also played an important role. There is evidence that the valley was at one time heavily forested—before the coming of the American settler. After the 1840s, with the building of homes and barns and especially after Yount and Bale built their sawmills, the forest lands began to diminish. Redwoods along the western side of the valley were the main source of building material, which may account for the fact that so many early barns and dwellings still stand intact. Pines and firs were also lumbered, and digger pines mostly for fuel. The many tanbark oaks were useful in tanning hides and skins.

Some redwoods are still to be found in quantity, mostly in the Las Posadas Forest on Howell Mountain, in the Lyman Canyon, and on the northern slopes of the Mayacmas. Bad fires have decimated the douglas firs and pines, however.

The earliest lumber outfit in the valley was the Napa Wood Company, which specialized in shipping firewood to San Francisco in the 1860s. Shipping poles was at one time a busy industry in Calistoga, the railroad being a ready loading point.

SETTLERS were sparse in Calistoga's rural areas, however, until after the 1880s. It will take much time and much more research, much digging to uncover the history of the people who started reaching out into the several districts surrounding Calistoga in the latter 1800s; but the results will be very much worthwhile and some day may be recorded for posterity, just as Elizabeth Wright and Burt Adams did with their stories of early Calistoga.

To obtain information about Porter Creek, which is the highlands above town and over the western ridge of the Mayacmas, I asked Everett Fechter of the long-time Fechter family residing there to help me. His findings point toward a fascinating story of that area and the various families who have lived there many years and have become active in civic and business affairs of the upvalley.

The first known settler in Porter Creek was Jerry Porter, who is believed to have come here in the 1850s and established a home about one mile up what is now Sharp Road, going toward the old picnic area of Heidelberg. In the troubled era when the U. S. government was trying to untangle the various claims under the Mexican land grants, "Porter's fields" was entered on the records in connection with another claim. This was in 1862. Alice Sharp Martin now lives on the former Porter ranch.

Next came Molly and Christopher Klotz, who obtained a patent from the U.S. government in 1872—the property now known as the Myers-Jensen place. Amelia Klotz, their daughter, married David Sharp, who bought a portion of the Porter ranch in 1906. A son, Herman, lived in Tucker District on the present Will Drew ranch.

The year before the Klotzes came, Charley Evans Peterson, the famous "Petrified Charley" who lived "in the strange forest of stone redwoods", made his discovery of the fallen giants while clearing off his pastureland. This was in 1871. His sister, Cristina Ryden, and her daughter, "Petrified Lizzie", kept house for him. The daughter, who used to teach music in Napa Valley, married O. G. Rohl. The Petrified Forest was made famous by Robert Louis Stevenson in "Silverado Squatters".

Also settling in Porter Creek prior to 1880, Everett found, were M. M. Carter, Irene Carter's father, on what is now the Dr. John Humber place; Lorenz Petersen, Milton Petersen's grandfather, on the present McComish ranch; Thomas Turner, whose daughter Harriett became Oliver Mangis' mother; the Hicklans, on the present site of the Triple S Ranch; and the Condra family, who owned property at the end of the Mountain Home Ranch road. Frank Moors bought both the Hicklan and Condra properties in 1896.

John Henry Fechter, Raymond Fechter's grandfather, acquired land in Porter Creek about 1895. A family named Lotridge, believed to be relatives of the Turners, also owned two parcels of land here at one time.

In the 1870s there was a sawmill above Heidelberg, but no one can recall the owner, says Everett.

TO the east and north of town lies King's Canyon, the steep, green terrain below the Palisades and Cathedral

Aerial view of the Palisades above Calistoga. Photo by Ted Miller

Rock. It is still rugged, at times almost impassable country and was named for a man named King who mined there at one time. In 1875 a Horace I. Weller staked out his "California claim" in the canyon, where other mines were located, including the Ida Easley, the Hellen and the Elephant.

Closer to the mountain and near the boundary line of the George Radelfinger ranch is another steep canyon known as Jericho, where there still may be seen the foundation stones of a building of some kind. Before John Lawley built the Toll Road, the way up the mountain lay through this canyon.

JAMES N. Bennett, who arrived in 1859, was the first to settle in the valley district north of town which bears his name. Adjoining his ranch were the Thomas Walsh and Hopkins places. Walsh started working his farm and ranch in 1865. The Arthur Calverts now own the property.

Others who came in the 1850s included William Dinning, John Lawler, William A. Haskin and William Moore; George Hoover, who bought one hundred and twenty acres west of town in 1856; and the Reverend J. M. Wright, who planted a fruit orchard and vineyard the same year. Historian Lyman L. Palmer writes that "the Rev. Mr. Wright published in 1878 'The Giant Mystery Explained: the Bible Teaches Three Distinct Original Creations of the Human Family'."

Feige reservoir, city's first source of water supply, filling for the first time, in 1886.

Palmer also notes that Martin E. Cook and Rufus Ingalls filed title to 2,559 acres in the northwestern part of Rancho Mallacomes in 1855.

IN the 1860s came Andrew Safley, W. P. de Boyce, J. Cook, Jackson G. Randall, and Amos Simmons. Safley, who had a degree in mechanics from Edinburgh University, bought farm land from Sam Brannan northwest of town, part of which is now owned by the Ben Sharpsteens. Safley's daughter Agnes married William F. Fisher, early stagecoach owner and founder of Calistoga's water works. De Boyce settled in Knight's Valley, in 1866, and two years later moved to town to become constable and deputy sheriff. Cook, who drove stage to Harbin Hot Springs in 1865, later opened a saloon and fruit stand in town. Randall bought a portion of the Ralph L. Kilburn grant two miles east of Calistoga in 1862 and planted fruit trees and grapes. That property is now owned by Milton and Barbara Eisele. Simmons planted a vineyard near town in 1864.

In the 1870s, J. C. and R. C. Bounsall set up a hardware store on Lincoln Avenue; S. W. Collins had a four-hundred acre ranch one mile west of town; Porter Decker had a stage and livery stable; and Louis Haeckl, who came to town in 1873, had a stationery store about where the second-hand shop is now located on Lincoln Avenue. Above his store were rooms, which he rented. This was the Star Hotel.

An early burial site in Calistoga was on the Greer property near the Lake County Highway just beyond Oat Hill Road turnoff and the present Louis Cravea produce stand.

Nelda Lincoln Williamson, whose mother was Grace Lane Lincoln, believes this cemetery was built in the early 1870s. The Lincoln family had a ranch across from the junction of the Lake County road and the Lawley Toll Road.

It was Collins who established what is now Pioneer Cemetery in 1877. Len Bryant of Porter Creek says his grandfather, Rev. Henry Doty Bryant, was the first one buried there. In 1936, Mrs. Annie Hopper, Collins' daughter, gave the cemetery to the city at the behest of C. L. Petersen, who was Memorial Day chairman here for several years.

The Holmes family Evergreen Cemetery in Knight's Valley is part of Rancho Mallacomes. It was established in 1883 by Calvin and Elvira Holmes when their daughter Kate died following the birth of her sixth child, George Foote.

THE story of Franz Valley is also fascinating—though a little involved—history.

Captain Frederick W. Franz, who is mentioned above, acquired his deed to the area in 1875 from Calvin H. and Thomas N. Blair and Phineas H. Wood, who in turn had bought this portion of the old Jose Santos Berryessa Rancho from William Elliott.

Franz' wife was the former Sarah Swarthout (same family as Gladys Swarthout, the famous opera and radio mezzo-soprano). Mrs. Franz' mother, Mary Sims Silbert, also acquired acreage in the valley: two parcels from military men who had been given "bounty land" as payment for their service during the Civil War, and one a patent from the state of California. The first two were for one-hundred-and-sixty acres each; the third for fifty-eight acres.

Franz' daughter Minnie married Samuel Davis Clark in 1883. They had four children: Valley V.; David; Halloween, who married Fred Popp, a mechanic-manager for Bill Spiers when the latter had his electricity plant in town and who later was to build his own concrete-block garage at Washington and Lincoln; and Lettie, who married Jack Fraser and, when he died, Lawrence Simmons.

Edith, who was Captain Franz' step-daughter, married George Wallace Kettlewell. The couple had a large family, eight children: William Wallace, Edith Daisy, Richard Stanley (Joe Kettlewell and Edith Baptie's father), Chester Arthur, Benjamin Barnett, Mamie Eliza, Jessie Lee and George Paul (Wally Kettlewell's father).

Their descendants – Edith Baptie and Joe and Wally Kettlewell and their families — still live in the valley. Clara, George Jr.'s widow, lives in town.

Jessie first married a Washabaugh, who died, and then Robert Sylvester. Richard Kettlewell, who gave me much of the history of Franz Valley, says that the Sylvesters bought the old Simmons place. This latter property had once belonged to J. P. Simmons, who had obtained from Mrs. Silbert in 1881 a right-of-way for a private road through her holdings to his own ranch, up in the hilly country on the western rim of the valley.

Richard tells me that he and his aunt, Edith Baptie, are now researching the history and biography of the valley and its people, most of the original written story of early settlers there having been burned up in the disastrous 1964 fire.

Sam and the Indian Hot Springs

NTO the easy-going frontier way of life there stepped the most fascinating man the upvalley had ever known. He touched it with magic, and it has never been the same since.

The man was Samuel Brannan, erstwhile Mormon and down-east Yankee printer who had "pulled himself up by his boot-straps" and his wits to become one of the best-known pioneers in the burgeoning former Mexican province of California. Already had he amassed his fortune, already made his mark for history. The year was 1852, and Sam was only 33.

One can imagine the impression the tall, handsome stranger had on the valley homesteaders, even though they may not have been quite so sure about his peculiar fascination with the Indian potholes and their steamy marshes.

Brannan could not help but be tremendously impressed by his first visit to the hot springs, the mecca which had drawn him here as though by magnet. Even so, Sam must have made an incongruous though resplendent figure, with his tight buff trousers, brocaded waistcoat, heavy gold watch chain, maybe even the elaborately carved leather holster with the pistol and bowie knife he was fond of wearing, as he edged closer to the hot, steamy turf of the Springs Ground.

In the cool, still air the warm vapors climbed and swirled, misting the outlines of a closely wooded hill just beyond. Above the mists and far off on the high horizon, in spectacular glory, a row of scraggy rocks cut across the northeastern sky; and in the cinnabar haze a sprawling mountain towered massively in the northwest.

Brannan drew a deep, appreciative breath. His friend, James M. Estill of Napa, and others had told him much about these springs, but he was hardly prepared for this. After all his restless wanderings, here was just what he was seeking. Never in all his colorful experiences had he found such natural beauty, such marvelous opportunity. Already his vision was leaping

Springs Ground and Mount Lincoln

ahead to the enormous possibilities, to what he, Sam Brannan, could do with all this.

Through the mists he could see rising a great spa, such a remarkable health resort that it would rival the famed Saratoga Hot Springs of New York and the watering spots of Europe. He had seen them all and he knew he could do it—only he would do better. And he had the means.

Already there were rumblings about a resort in the planning for a place downvalley at the springs located in 1848 by David Hudson, near what we now call St. Helena. But Sam had encountered and bested competition before.

Sam Brannan: California pioneer, soldier-of-fortune, newspaper publisher, friend of tycoons and royalty, legendary saint and sinner, already enormously wealthy—how had such a man decided to come to the frontier wilderness of a northern California valley?

The saga of Sam Brannan is the story of a star which rose like a shining meteor, flamed across the California sky for three decades, and fell, just as suddenly, just as dramatically.

It had always been said of Sam Brannan that he was born lucky. He always seemed "to be there" when important things were about to happen. Not only that: he also had the God-given talent for knowing what to do with his opportunities. Perhaps that Irish ancestry of his had something to do with it.

Brannan has been described as tall and darkly handsome, with full, passionate lips and bold, romantic eyes, his bearing self-assured, almost debonair. James Scherer in "The Golden Tea Caddy" calls Brannan "the first '49er, the original Californiac, barrel-chested, broad-shouldered, dark-eyed and dark-haired, his extremely bland features masculined with side-burns", but as yet without the heavy whiskers he affected later in life. "His manners were coarse and his speech bombastic; but he was courageous and generous to a fault. A canny Yankee trader, Sam was a real spieler with a powerful, penetrating voice. He was master of the punch line" and much given to making speeches from balconies. "In other words, he was 'coarse gold' —unrefined but, like his age, dramatic, heroic, Homeric."

What, then, had brought such a man to the hot springs?

STRANGELY enough, it was Mormon money which was indirectly responsible for the founding of Calistoga; for it was Mormon money which got Sam started. He was born in Saco, Maine, in 1819, the son of Tom Brannan, former Waterford, Ireland, farmer, and had early learned the printer's trade in Ohio. By 1842 he had adopted the Mormon faith in order to become the publisher of a Mormon newspaper in New York.

Meanwhile, back in the Midwest, trouble was brewing for the Latter Day Saints, finally erupting into open violence when their prophet, Joseph Smith, was murdered by a mob. Brigham Young and Brannan, who by now was an elder, were named to head an expedition away from hostile Americans and into the western wilderness in search of a new home for the sect.

Opportunity was knocking for young Brannan. Young went overland with his band, and Sam chose to go by sea, around the Cape, in the chartered ship *Brooklyn*. By 1846 they had reached the Sandwich Islands, better known in those days than California, since they were a whaling and watering stop between China and the ports of New York and Boston.

However the *Brooklyn* carried guns and ammunition; and since these were not allowed in the Islands, King Kamehameha forbade their landing. The ship went on to Yerba Buena.

The tiny waterfront settlement had only about fifty inhabitants at that time. The *Brooklyn* carried two-hundred and thirty-six, including women and children! Nothing daunted—

and because Yerba Buena had just been taken over from the Spaniards by the Americans, from whom the Mormons were fleeing—most of the newcomers spread out into northern California, to the Sacramento area, and Sam along with them, although he did keep his ties with the new town on the bay. Sam was on his way.

He settled his colonists on the first farm in the fertile San Joaquin valley and at Mormon Island near Sacramento. He had brought with him from the East a printing press, type, a stock of paper, machinery for making flour mills and various agricultural implements. By 1847, Brannan had set himself up in the mercantile business at Natoma, which he renamed Coloma, after an Indian chief, Cuuloma, and had also bought a one-thousand acre ranch on the Feather River. Through friendship and business relations with the Swiss adventurer John Augustus Sutter, who had a flourishing shipping trade between New Helvetia and the port of Yerba Buena, Brannan was soon becoming influential in the economic life of northern California. Yerba Buena itself had by now been renamed "San Francisco."

With Brannan and other pioneers, Sutter was later to found Sacramento. He had obtained his huge land possessions —some one-hundred-and-fifteen square miles in the Sacramento and San Joaquin valleys — through treaties with the Indians, in Mexican land grants, and by purchase of the Russian holdings at the Fort of the Russians (Fort Ross).

By 1849 the pueblo of San Francisco had grown into a sizeable city, with hotels, commercial buildings, restaurants, gambling houses and bars—all notwithstanding its muddy streets which became bogs in winter. Sam had started his *California Star* newspaper and, as usual, was in the thick of things, an entrepreneur in everything from gambling to banking.

Sam's virtue had always been that he "started things", never counting the cost to himself or his possessions. Yet he was to say years later he considered the real high point of his career was "founding of the Committee of Vigilance", the Vigilantes, to "combat the incendiarism and lawlessness" which plagued the booming town of San Francisco. (Historians have disputed the Vigilantes' integrity: they numbered among their members too many with past criminal careers and, even after their organizing, were guilty of murdering innocent men, it was held.)

History shows that Sam Brannan did not mind resorting to a little shady deal himself, however; for example, his method of obtaining money with which to finance his many schemes. He would rent a "stick-and-canvas shack" along Market Street in the City for $600 to $1,000 a month; he borrowed money cheaply in New York and lent it out in San Francisco at twelve percent; he charged high interest rates for money advanced in title litigation; he bought up property at " distress prices" from those who thought they might lose; and he even sold the Mormon farm in the San Joaquin valley and kept the proceeds.

As Mormon elder, he had always collected thirty per cent of the "take" of his Mormon Battalion workers as "the Lord's tithes"; but he had not sent this back to the head of the church at Salt Lake. Instead, Sam Brannan had invested the tithes for himself, in real estate and other ventures.

When Young heard of this latter, he sent an apostle to collect. Characteristically, Sam roared, "I'll give up the Lord's money when he sends me a receipt signed by the Lord—and no sooner!"

Scherer adds that Brannan was disfellowshipped from the Mormon Church.

SAM was the first to tell the world about the discovery of gold at Sutter's mill, where many of his Mormons were working. Brannan is reported to have rushed to San Francisco, beaver hat in hand, "wildly waving a flashing flask" of gold dust and bellowing, "Gold! Gold! Gold from the American River!"

Others, more in spite and envy perhaps than not, said Sam had waited to buy up all the merchandise in Sacramento and San Francisco before announcing his discovery. It was May 11, 1848, a few months, actually, after the precious metal had first been discovered.

But Sam Brannan himself did not go into the gold fields. Instead, he waited for the gold to come to him. In fact, gold dust came in so fast to Sam's store that he simply poured the dust into chamber pots beneath the counters. Soon he had four stores—the only ones for miles around. With these and because of his sound real-estate investments, Sam was fast becoming the first millionaire in California.

He looked around for more worlds to conquer. Restless, he took his wife, Ann Eliza, and four children—Sam Jr., Adelaide, Fanny and Lisa—to Europe, where he visited various spas and also enrolled the children in schools on the continent. Back in the States Sam had visited the famed Saratoga Hot Springs in New York, and now he not only went to the best of European spas; he also had begun scheming again, possibly for one of his own.

By 1851 he was shipping back home, to his farm in the Sacramento Valley or to his Hawaiian possessions, blooded sheep from Spain, choice French and Italian grape cuttings, and Arabian horses, also from Spain.

In another of his extraneous schemes, Sam and several California businessmen, including his Napa friend Estill, had become owners of several choice parcels on Oahu and a sugar plantation on Kauai. In fact, they were even planning to annex the Sandwich Islands to the United States. King Kamehameha, however, wasn't exactly a "pushover." He complained about the scheme to the federal government, which had no desire to make war on the doughty Islanders, as the Californians were urging. Instead, Sam and his wealthy friends were warned not to proceed with their plans but to sell all their holdings in the Islands and stay away from there.

And so Sam needed another outlet for those tremendous energies. Estill and others were urging that he look at the wilderness hot springs north of Napa. And Sam became interested, determined to see for himself why professional and wealthy elite were so much interested in the Napa Valley.

He came by boat to Vallejo and by carriage to the upvalley hot springs. The rest is history.

BRANNAN laid his plans carefully, and by 1859 the Yankee trader was ready to fulfill his dreams of a "Saratoga of the Pacific."

He purchased about 2,000 choice acres of upvalley property, including the wonderful Indian hot springs, and proceeded to pour thousands of dollars into it despite dire warnings from his frugal brother John: "all valley land, including all the warm springs", Apr. 6, 1857, for $10, from Martha H. Ritchie; ditto, Sept. 24, 1859, for $10,000, from Henry Edgerton; four square leagues, Mar. 6, 1862, for $25,000, from J. S. Berryessa et als.; from Henry Fowler et ux., Apr. 29, 1863, 1,000 acres for $1,200. (Hall of Records' entries)

By 1860 the first main building, the Hot Springs Hotel, had been built and on a lavish scale for those days. By the time the entire resort opened in 1862, twenty-five five-roomed cottages had also been constructed, each with a veranda, some with scalloped trim dripping from their eaves, others with mansard roofs and "gingerbread" decoration.

(Robert Louis Stevenson, who occupied one of these in 1880, vividly describes them and the resort layout in his "Silverado Squatters.")

A Sam Brannan cottage

Burt Adams lists the names of some of these which were retained by private individuals, as "summer retreats": Tehama, Occidental, Revere, Waverly and Woodward, all along Palm Row, as Adams called it; Winans, Lindell, Metropolitan on Wapoo Avenue between Lincoln and Grant; and Ralston, St. Nicholas, Garrison and Reis on Wapoo north of Grant.

For his grand opening Brannan had chartered a ship to bring guests from San Francisco to Suscol, the water connection at that time with Vallejo. They were met by carriages and stage coaches which brought them up the valley to the resort, where special guests were treated to a lavish spread of roast meats and fowl, delicacies of the season and champagne; and a huge barbecue, complete with barrelsful of beer, entertained the throngs outside.

Brannan indeed had something to celebrate: with Mount St. Helena as a grand backdrop to the former Indian Coo-lay-no-maock, Sam had laid out a beautiful extravaganza of wide circular avenues; elaborately landscaped parks dotted with bathing pavilions shaped like miniature pagodas; the Hot Springs Hotel gleaming white at the foot of Mount Lincoln with a broad, tree-lined avenue leading to its front steps; the handsome two-story Mansion House nearby; cottage clusters and a bathhouse; a huge skating rink and dance pavilion; and high above it all, atop the hundred-foot Mount Lincoln itself, a tent-shaped observatory with wide walkways and reached by a long flight of wooden stairs whence visitors could get a magnificent view of the entire countryside.

Beneath the observatory was a large, 90,000-gallon reservoir to hold water for the resort. Adams says that a steam pump raised water from a nearby "creek"—possibly the Napa River or a tributary.

Old prints of Brannan's dream resort also show a big store at Wapoo and Grant, an express office, a swimming pool, a goldfish pond with a Druidical temple above it, and, to the north and west, another forty acres enclosing a mile-long race track and stables. The temple itself, says Adams, was fifteen feet high and twenty-five feet in circumference. It and a fence surrounding the main concourse had been built with petrified wood brought from the Petrified Forest five miles distant on the Santa Rosa road. Several stumps can still be seen on the grounds of Pacheteau's Original Hot Springs.

PROMINENTLY affixed to one of these is a bronze plaque dedicated to Sam Brannan in 1954 by E

Clampus Vitus, fraternal social organization whose members memorialize the traditions, personalities and places rich in early California and Nevada history.

(I am indebted to several Clampers—including Hobart M. "Ick" Lovett of San Francisco and Jess Doud of Napa, both members of the Yerba Buena Chapter; and Ed Hawkins and Conrad Weil of the Sam Brannan Napa County chapter—for information about the organization.)

E Clampus Vitus came from western Virginia to the Mother Lode in 1849-50 as "a caricature of the standard lodge, for the purpose of providing relief to widows and orphans," a local Clamper told me. Chapters sprang up in several mining towns and even spread to San Francisco. There is no record of Sam's being a Clamper, though as Doud tells me, "he certainly would have been a good one—a humdinger!"

More or less dormant since Gold Rush days, E Clampus Vitus was again resurrected in 1931 in San Francisco by Carl I. Wheat and Adam Lee Moore. The Napa County chapter, Hawkins says, has been very active. In addition to the Sam Brannan plaque, the lodge has also recently dedicated Pioneer Cemetery, in 1975; the Masonic Temple in St. Helena, in 1976; and March 19, 1977, the Old Adobe at the intersection of Soscol and Silverado Trail. One of the few remaining adobe structures in the county, the Old Adobe was built by Don Cayetano Juarez in 1840 as part of his original Mexican land grant, Rancho Tulocay. It is now a popular luncheon spot.

In response to my query as to the meaning of the singular name, Lovett's tongue-in-cheek explanation is this: "E Clampus Vitus is a derivation of the medieval ecclesiastical expression 'Ecce, Lampas Vitae, Behold, the Torch of Life.' And further: 'Per Caritate Viduaribus Orphanibusque sed Prime Viduaribus. For the Benefit of Widows and Orphans but Primarily of Widows!"

Sam Brannan. Dreamer, Promoter, Prince of Californiacs. Here in 1859 he created the name "Calistoga." Dedicated Oct. 24, 1954, by E Clampus Vitus.

43

OUNT Lincoln today is overgrown with cactus and other vegetation; but those willing to climb to the top can still find the hole where Sam's observatory-reservoir once stood. The hole is partially filled with dirt and rubbish. The structure itself burned down July 4, 1877.

While I was doing research at the Calistoga Library, librarian Katherine Boyadjieff brought me a well-illustrated reference book, "Handbook of the Calistoga Springs", which was published in San Francisco by the *Alta California* Book and Job Printing House, 1871. It contains a clear drawing of four structures along the railroad: a brandy distillery, a cooper's shop, a refinery and a depot. Brannan co-owned the distillery with Lewis Keseberg, a survivor of the Donner Party. The railroad depot, which was added after the others, still stands today. It is this State Historic Monument No. 687, which Milton and Vera Petersen and associates are restoring as a feature of the "Calistoga Depot" complex.

At one time, by the way, in the late 1920s, a nine-hole golf course was laid out on the Springs Ground, with sand "greens."

Because the soil of the Hot Springs contained—then, as now—high concentrations of boron and other toxic minerals, Brannan had to bring in fresh soil for the many trees and shrubs which were to grace his resort grounds and also to develop agriculture to supply the many needs of the hotel and its guests.

Off to the west, Brannan set aside fifteen acres for a tea plantation, a mulberry grove to grow silkworms, and choice grape vines, bringing in Japanese labor especially to tend these experiments. Neither the mulberry grove nor the tea plantation ever amounted to much; the vines, however, prospered, as they do today all over the valley.

One of the features of the resort in later years came to be known as the "Chicken Broth Spring," which was one of the lathed-over miniature geysers which abounded on the Springs Ground and gave it its name.

All one had to do, Adams writes, was "add a pinch of salt and a dash of pepper." He says he himself often boiled eggs in its waters. A sign above the spring read, "The Devil's Kitchen. Cook for Yourself."

In addition to his resort and to help supply the needs of that spa, Brannan also laid out a new town across the Springs Ground to the south and west and separated into two parts by the "creek" or "crick", as early residents came to call Napa River, which "came down from the shoulders of the mountain and rambled on downvalley to bisect it, too," Robert Louis Stevenson was to write in his "Silverado Squatters." The famous Scot roughed in that book while living a short time on the Springs Ground and later on the mountain itself.

For many years, before the railroad left and Lincoln Avenue was extended across the Light vineyard to the north of town, Calistoga had essentially the same layout as Brannan gave it: a residential twelve square blocks between Main Street and the "creek"; and a commercial and resort area on the other. Joining the Springs Ground and Main Street was Lincoln Avenue, which Stevenson was to call "High Street" in "The Squatters." Sam engaged Tom Morgan to draw the map of his town, still today the basic map of the township, though much changed in parts. (See end papers.)

The Brannan stables, which at one time attracted blooded horses and their wealthy owners — such names as Hopkins, Hearst, Lick and Leland Stanford—, still stands on Grant Street, across from Stevenson. The building is essentially the same as in Brannan's day, except for the stucco exterior. Ephraim Light converted the interior into a winery when he bought the property; and later it became the Napa Valley Cooperative Winery.

(Light also moved the Brannan winery from where it stood beside the creek near Brannan Street to a site below the present Harwood Allen place on the Trail and converted it into a home for his family. It is now part of the Louis Navone ranch.)

HARDLY had his resort become a reality than Sam was busy with plans for still another adventure, this time a railroad to bring visitors to his resort.

However, Sam's flamboyance and ruthlessness in his dealings with his neighbors had already made him unpopular with the early settlers, who, after all, were farmers and stock men and had become well-established before he came along.

The promoter allowed his imported sheep to run at

large in the northeast foothills, intruding on settlers' crops and spoiling the cattlemen's pasturage.

When approached about this, Brannan shrugged his shoulders and said, "Build yourselves some fences!"

Finally, realizing they could get nowhere with Brannan, several young men of the countryside got together one night in 1867 and went "'coon hunting". By morning they had killed off Brannan's prized Merinos.

Sam was "wild and had nearly everyone arrested", according to Adams. There was a long court trial, but nothing ever came of it; and, while Brannan fumed for a while, he was never able to do anything more about it.

Another day, in a dispute over a sawmill on which he had lent money, Sam was shot eight times by a man named Snyder and seriously wounded. A bullet in his left hip left him partially paralyzed the rest of his life.

Nothing daunted, Sam recovered and went ahead with his plans for the railroad.

THE long, mournful whistle of the train tracking up and down the valley will always be a colorful memory of Napa Valley dwellers. But there was a time when mere mention of a railroad here was enough to stir up a hornet's nest.

It was during the war between the states that Brannan and a group of prominent business and civic leaders of the county

got together to spearhead the financing and building of a railroad from the Bay Area to the then unsettled upper end of the Napa Valley in order to develop that area. The Napa Valley Railroad Company was incorporated March 26, 1864, to build from Suscol on the Napa River northward to Calistoga.

Following an okeh by the governor and the legislature, the county's electorate voted the necessary $225,000 to build the railroad and purchase the stock. Many individuals, including Brannan, who gave $8,000, donated money or property rights-of-way to help the project.

July 11, 1865, the first train passed over the track, completed to Main and Third streets in Napa from Suscol, head of navigation on the river, where passengers could take the steamer to San Francisco. Rolling stock consisted of two cars, with a capacity of one-hundred-and-five passengers, and a pony engine. The latter was replaced by a new $9,000 locomotive in November.

But after six months of operation, the hard facts of dollars and cents sobered taxpayers' dreams of building an empire through the railroad. Interest alone ate up half the profits. Too, the section of the road already built had cost more than had been anticipated; and another bond issue would have to be floated to complete the road to Calistoga. Partisanship grew over the railroad question: "How could a train to the wilderness of the upvalley pay for itself when the present facility wasn't making money?", asked an editorial in *The Napa Register*, county newspaper. "The whole county would have to be taxed for the benefit of the few," it went on, meaning, of course, Sam Brannan, who by this time was sinking a fortune into his "Saratoga of the Pacific."

A heavily signed petition against completing the railroad went to the legislature which, nevertheless, passed the second Napa County railroad bill, calling for another election.

Passage of the bill fell like a bombshell. *The Register* urged votes against the "scheme," which would "surely bring bankruptcy and ruin upon every taxpayer and his family."

The bonds were defeated by a conclusive majority.

Undaunted, friends of the railroad pushed another bill through the legislature in September 1866, providing for another election to decide whether the railroad should have donated to it the entire amount of the first bond issue or whether a macadamized road should be built up the valley. By this time the voters were either too befuddled by the whole scheme or felt that the bonds would go by default anyway; and they failed to show up at the polls.

The macadamized-road project failed, and the Supreme Court was called upon to force the Board of Supervisors —who were refusing to float new bonds—to issue $194,000 in bonds.

In September 1867 the second section opened to Oakville; on to St. Helena in February 1868 and to Calistoga in August of that year.

On its completion Sam Brannan was sufficiently recovered from his near brush with death in the sawmill affair to play host to a grand excursion to his newly opened resort at Calistoga. Three thousand visitors are said to have come to partake of the pioneer's lavish hospitality. And, contrary to prophets of doom, the railroad finally did prosper—for the time being, anyway.

A final section from Suscol southward to Napa Junction on the California Pacific, which by this time had built a mainline from south Vallejo to Sacramento and Suisun, was opened in January 1869. However, this company went under foreclosure in May and eventually was transferred, June 9, 1869, to the California Pacific Railroad Extension Company. The latter firm had taken title to the Napa Valley Railroad between Napa Junction and Calistoga, a distance of thirty-five miles, in April. In turn, the California Pacific Railroad Extension and the California Pacific were consolidated in December as the California Pacific.

With the sale of the Napa Valley Railroad to the California Pacific for $500,000, the pioneer chapter of one of the most interesting facets of the valley's story of transportation came to an end.

By July 1, 1876, the Central Pacific had acquired the railroad lease. The line was in turn leased to the Southern Pacific, Central's successor, in 1885; and in 1898 the road became part of the "SP".

(Data on the railroad story is from Palmer's "History of Napa and Lake Counties" and also from "Western Railroader.")

Incidentally, Petersen and his associates have acquired

one of the original Central Pacific cars, to be made a part of the depot complex here.

THE successful building of his railroad project to Calistoga was the crowning point of Sam's career but also marked the end of his good luck. For, if Brannan's star of fortune had climbed steadily before his Calistoga adventure, it sank rapidly afterwards. In Scherer's words, "If a boom town built his fortune, a boom town turned his luck." The intrepid entrepreneur whose touch had once turned everything to gold suddenly lost that Midas gift. The man who had published the first newspaper in San Francisco, who had actually helped found both Sacramento and San Francisco, who at one time was said to have owned one-fourth of the first and one-fifth of the second, who was first president of both the Society of California Pioneers and the Sam Brannan Committee of Vigilance, who had been instrumental in building the first railroad in California and even headed his own bank and issued his own bank notes (a common practice for banks, companies and communities from the 1830s until the end of the Civil War)—incredibly, that man was "broke."

Enemies began to whisper that Sam's "only success was his distillery, and he was his own best customer."

Sam's enchantment with the lovely dancer Lola Montez, "Firebelle Lillie" Hitchcock Coit and other women hadn't helped matters between him and his wife, Ann Eliza. His marriage, always a stormy one, was breaking up; and his family, including his son, Sam Jr., turned bitter toward him after their mother's divorce.

To make matters worse, his friend Leland Stanford, who had also invested a large sum in the Hot Springs, decided that Calistoga was too far from the metropolitan center of things and decided to site his university on the Peninsula, at Palo Alto. Stanford was especially strengthened in this resolve after another friend, James Lick, whom he had sent to reconnoiter the up-valley for a suitable site, had been summarily dumped into the water of a small creekbed when the stagecoach in which he was riding hit a boulder. Lick declared that the place was just "too uncivilized" for a university.

Sam's brother John had always objected to his brother's spending so much money in Calistoga, especially since Brannan had never been too careful about those he entrusted with his finances. John is reported to have told his brother, "Your manager took off with the cash and whatever else was portable," early in Sam's Calistoga venture.

Now, added to Brannan's financial losses, his marital infidelity and final separation from his wife and family, came a division of the estate. In 1870, after extended court proceedings, Ann Eliza was awarded one-half of community property; and Brannan had to liquidate almost everything he had.

Ann Eliza Brannan always wore "widow's weeds"
after her divorce from Sam.
Courtesy, Pete Molinari

Finally, by the end of 1873, Sam was ready to admit financial failure and leased the place to George Schonewald. Financial wizard though he was, Brannan was forced to admit that "it was his greatest business mistake (Calistoga) which eventually contributed to his financial downfall."

Too, between 1869 and 1875, other resorts, especially Napa Soda Springs, had set up in competition with Calistoga Hot Springs and had begun to take the place of the upvalley in attracting the wealthy and exclusive. Sam's Mansion House, on whose register had been written names like Mark Hopkins, C. P. Huntington, Lick and others, failed. It burned to the ground in 1879 and though rebuilt never regained its pristine glory.

June 5, 1875, the Sacramento Savings Bank, holder of the mortgage on the resort, ordered the sale of all of Brannan's property in Calistoga. All except the main resort, which was retained by Leland Stanford, and several cottages which were privately owned was sold in various-sized parcels. Stanford leased the property to others to manage; and the Hot Springs went through several hands, including Judge Elmer S. Dudley of Falls City, Nebraska, A. C. Tichenor of San Francisco, and eventually to Jacques Pacheteau about 1911. The resort is now operated as Pacheteau's Original Hot Springs, Inc.

At one time, famous stage coach driver and civic leader Bill Spiers considered leasing the property at the Springs Ground, but the deal fell through. However, Spiers did erect a beautiful redwood-log gate at the entrance. It has since been taken down.

Stanford's interests in the resort were sold in 1919, when the modern resort era here began.

MEANWHILE, although Sam Brannan had reluctantly given up his dreams of fame and fortune in his "Saratoga of the Pacific," in 1878, at the age of 60, he was to try to launch yet another career.

Back in the middle 1860s Sam had helped finance an

A redwood gate, constructed by Bill Spiers, once stood at the entrance to the Hot Springs.

expedition to repel Napoleon III in the latter's invasion of Mexico. In return for his generosity, the Mexican government had given Brannan some Mexican bonds. With these, he now obtained a land grant of 1,687,585 acres in Mexico and established the Sonora City and Improvement Company, incorporated under the laws of the state of New York. He even made surveys there for a railroad.

But it was not to be. Sam was everywhere thwarted in his efforts to take over the property and continually harassed by Yaqui Indians, who, after all, had been on the land long before Sam came. He finally had to give up his last attempt at an "empire."

Helped along by loans from his nephew, Alexander Badlam Jr., Sam even resorted at one time to peddling pencils to support himself. At the age of 69 and after an unsuccessful Mexican marriage, Sam went to live in southern California; and Magdalena Moraga, a Mexican woman, came to keep house for him.

Newspapers published accounts of the Mexican government's finally repaying Sam $49,000 interest on his loan, so that he was able to pay off his debts. But that item has been disputed, notably by biographer Reva Scott in "Samuel Brannan and the Golden Fleece."

Sam's last days were spent puttering around on his fig ranch in Escondido. Once so well known that billboards advertised products with the slogan "Sam Brannan Buys It!" and at one time "one of the most flamboyant dressers in San Francisco," the former millionaire was remembered for years only by an obscure street in San Francisco and by another in his other "boom town", Calistoga.

Biographer Scherer writes: "The Mormon renegade, drunkard, rake, always controversial but ever the adventurer finally quit his drinking, got rid of his paralysis and, when he died on May 6, 1889, was penniless but owed no man."

Sam had once dedicated an elaborate family burial plot in Calistoga, but he was destined never to occupy it, although an infant son and other members of the family did. Winans Vault, built with stones brought from China by Joseph W. Winans, can still be seen today to the rear of the Chance Ingalls' property on Foothill Blvd., site of the former home of Ezra T. Badlam, Sam's nephew. Winans married Sarah Badlam, Sam's niece.

Sixteen years after Sam's death, his nephew Alex bought a lot in Mount Hope Cemetery in San Diego and had Brannan buried there. His son, Sam Jr., from whom he had been estranged most of his life, is interred nearby.

The inscription on Sam's headstone reads:

BACK at the Hot Springs, all but one of the white cottages on the Springs Ground had been moved to other parts of town or had burned. That lone reminder of better days, with its tall palm and nearby stand of petrified wood, remained over the years as a feature of the resort. This cottage, California Registered Historical Monument No. 685, has now been moved to the Calistoga pioneer museum complex and restored by the city, with the aid of volunteer history "buffs."

Behind the cottage on Washington Street is a new museum, generously donated by Ben and Bernice Sharpsteen of the long-time Bennett District family. It houses a three-dimensional diorama of Brannan's Hot Springs and the early main section of town, complete with structures, landscaping and miniature people and animals, all built to scale by Ruth and Robert Durbin of Calistoga, under Sharpsteen's direction.

Ben, who formerly produced nature films for Walt Disney, tells me he regards the replication of Brannan's spa the high point of his long career! He was inspired to undertake the project, he says, when he saw John Ghisolfo's unique photographs of the Hot Springs, "possibly made in 1862." It is these four pictures, which Ghisolfo had the foresight to have restored, at considerable expense to himself, which served as a model for the museum diorama.

Working with Sharpsteen and the Durbins was artist Kendall O'Connor, also formerly with Disney, who painted the background murals and other scenes. A citizens' committee and the Napa Valley Heritage Fund were also involved in recreating Sam's "Saratoga of the Pacific."

The Sharpsteen place, by the way, is a part of the former Andrew Safley ranch, bought from Sam Brannan. Apple trees still producing were in the old family orchard, Ben says.

ANOTHER Brannan cottage can be seen on Wapoo, not far from Lincoln and different from Palm Row structures in that it has an intricate scroll work beneath its front gable rather than scallops on the veranda. It is better preserved, having been occupied most of the time since Brannan's day. Two characteristic palms stand on either side of the cottage, which is owned by Mabel Petersen, mother of realtor Milton Petersen.

A third cottage, complete with scalloped trim, was moved to Cedar Street, across from Pioneer Park, by Tom C. Brown in 1876. Like the Wapoo cottage, it has been remodeled inside and repainted several times, but it still retains much of its early charm. The Weddell place next door, now owned by the Elmer F. Hembergers, may also be a "Brannan."

Homes on Lake Street are still shaded today by the long row of elm trees Sam planted at his race track, and several palms and century plants he set out on the Springs Ground and observatory hill still thrive.

Brannan Street, which leads from Mount Lincoln to what was once Brannan Avenue or Vineyard Avenue (now the Silverado Trail), has recently been improved by the city.

Incidentally, there are two maps of early Calistoga hanging at the city hall on Washington Street: one made in 1866 by E. J. Dewoody and the other by Tom Morgan in 1871. A third map, dated April 20, 1877, may be seen on the wall of the recorder's office in the Hall of Records in Napa. It reads: "Map of Calistoga Lands as Surveyed in 1871 and Subdivided in Part in 1876" by order of the Sacramento Savings Bank. It bears many names well-known today, holders of property in various parts of the upvalley.

Sam's Legacy

DESPITE all Sam's troubles with pioneers and neighbors, Brannan's contribution to the upvalley had not gone unnoticed in the county as a whole. On the day of the shooting incident over the sawmill, *The Register* summed up his accomplishments: "Mr. Brannan has done more for Napa County than any other two men and has expended his money freely. He has developed the resources of the valley to the utmost, and, should his death follow his wounds, his place would not be filled. It is only now when death seems about to rob us of him that his good qualities are recognized and appreciated according to their merits."

Although the resort consumed a great deal of the crops and other products of the farms and ranches around it and independent farming was restricted, still Brannan must be recognized for eventually developing the town of Calistoga, which flourished as Sam's star faded. An instinctive and canny promoter to the end, Sam had always been able to attract others to the West Coast, to California. Before the Gold Rush, he had published a special edition of his *California Star*, extolling the attractions of the state, even packing off two-thousand copies aboard a mule train to Missouri to induce friends and relatives to come to California to build homes and stores. This at a time when postage cost fifty cents a letter!

Anxious for Calistoga to have its own newspaper, Brannan induced Thomas George, who was working on the *Alta California* in San Francisco, to come here in 1871 and start the community's first periodical, *The Tribune*. He and it died in 1873, however.

The following year O. P. Hoddy issued the first number of the *Free Press*, which was published weekly until October of 1875.

The Weekly Calistogian appeared April 6, 1876, edited by J. H. Upton. It ran for four months, to be followed by an amateur publication which was issued for sixteen months.

December 24, 1877, J. H. Multer issued the first number of the *Independent Calistogian*. He sold out to I. N. Bennett and

G. B. Douglass in 1892.

It was in June, 1895, that C. A. Carroll, the twenty-two-year-old former editor of the *Mendocino Beacon*, purchased the paper, married a local school teacher, Mertie Bennett, and with her published the paper, now called the *Weekly Calistogan*, until his death in 1946. Their daughter, Lois Carroll Winston, and her husband Ralph later took over publication.

I joined the staff in 1956 and helped put out the paper until 1962. It is now owned and published by Libby-Brandon, Inc.

THE newspaper was only one of many enterprises Sam Brannan helped establish. At first most of these were satellites of the resort. When Sam left, they gradually became more and more independent, and Lincoln Avenue soon had homes and prospering businesses from the railroad to Main Street, and about five-hundred residents.

Among establishments here in Brannan's day were the Ayers' dairy ranch; Kong Sam Kee's Chinese laundry; Henry Gettleson and Morris Friedberg's merchandise store at Lincoln and Washington; a string of Chinese coolie shacks facing the railroad tracks and housing laborers who were building the railroad; Woodward's store and post office near Hazel and Main; G. B. Clifford's Lodi Stables; DeLosh's Mountain House at Main and Hazel; the Chesebro saloon and Magnolia Hotel on Lincoln in mid-town Calistoga; the Eagle Fruit Store across from the railroad station; R. S. Feige's saddlery and harness shop; Judge A. C. Palmer's planing mill on Washington, with a footbridge across the "creek" to his home on Cedar Street; Towle and Sons' grocery; Sam Chapman's wagon and carriage factory on the bank of the river, about opposite the present city hall; M. B. Kelley, shoes; and Brown and Easley's blacksmith shop.

Always generous, Sam gave away lots to Mary Ayer, Mattie C. Gesford, J. W. Norton, Andrew Safley, several Badlams (his relatives on his older sister Mary's side), Sarah A. Winans, his niece, William Fisher and more than eighty others, encouraging them to build homes and start businesses in his new town.

He also donated land for a church, the Methodist-Episcopal denomination. No sooner had the foundation been laid, however, than the railroad decided the land was needed for a depot and tracks; and so Sam gave the church another lot, this one at Cedar and Spring streets. The church building was completed in 1869. The structure has been used since by several denominations, currently the Jehovah's Witnesses, the Methodists having joined with the Presbyterians in 1946 to form Calistoga Federated Church, at Third and Washington streets. (In 1959 the name was changed to the Calistoga Community Church.)

Incidentally, the first religious services in the valley by a regular preacher were held in 1851 at Napa by the Reverend Samuel D. Simonds, a Methodist minister. The Reverend Asa White came to the upvalley in 1852 and preached in the "blue-tent church" in a redwood grove donated by Reasin Tucker. The following year pioneers built the famous "White Church", which was 22 feet x 32 feet in size, with Dr. L. G. Lillie supplying the lumber. The building had two entrances—one for women, the other for men, who sat on opposite sides of the church. The building is gone now, but the cemetery behind it—believed to be the oldest public cemetery in the valley—still exists, despite efforts of vandals to despoil it.

EARLY on, Sam recognized the great natural wealth of the hot mineral waters here, which are full of sulphur, iron, magnesia and other chemicals. It was on the Springs Ground that the first shooting geyser started spouting—and that accidentally. Workmen were boring a well in front of the Mansion House in the 1860s. Suddenly, at a depth of sixty-five feet, the instruments were blown out with tremendous force high into the air. The workmen ran for their lives and could not be induced to return. When an attempt was made to pump water out of the hole, a violent stream of hot water blew out, more than twenty feet high.

Bancroft's Tourist Guide about 1868 told how the neighborhood suspected that the "diabolus ipse", the "devil himself", was at work underground in Calistoga, especially since there was quite a "prevailing and Stygian odor" from the place.

57

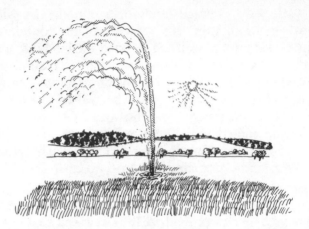

Stevenson, when he came here a few years later, described Calistoga as "lying above a boiling, subterranean lake."

Adams says that apparently nothing more was done about that attempt to bore a well there. "The probabilities are that it was filled with debris and forgotten," he adds.

The Light geyser was the first of the modern spouters, drilled in 1918. Ephraim Light, whose winery was the former Brannan stables, engaged Frank Strubel to drill a well in order to obtain hot water to wash out the wine barrels and tanks. At one-hundred-and-fifty feet water was struck. Workmen left for the day.

About midnight Ephraim's son Ed, who lived in the former Brannan store at Wapoo and Grant, heard a loud, swishing noise. The boiling water had burst through the temporary cover and was tumbling high up into the air. Thus was born the famous Light geyser, which brought hundreds to sightsee. Finally, because increasing crowds kept interfering with wine-making, the Lights had the geyser capped, allowing spouting only on Sundays.

Anyone who has watched the Old Faithful Geyser of Tubbs Lane spout (which it does regularly) may experience the same thrill as that which people from all over had when they came here of a Sunday to picnic and watch the Light geyser erupting. Occasionally the Pacheteau geyser between the bathhouse and the swimming tank is allowed to erupt, a really beautiful sight. However, most of the time it is kept under control so as not to lower too much the available underground supply of hot water for the nearby bathhouses.

Y 1874 the pioneer period was over, and the town was pretty well established. Business structures lined both sides of Lincoln Avenue from the railroad to the river, and side streets were being built up with comfortable homes. The L. M. Corwin census of 1880 lists 1,259 residents.

Suddenly, on a hot August afternoon in 1901, everything came to a tragic halt. A small quantity of gasoline stored behind John L. Wolfe's grocery exploded. Immediately the town became one vast inferno. Men who rushed to help others save their stores returned home to find their own places in flames. Thelma Tamagni has an old clipping from the August 2, 1901, San Francisco *Call* with the headline: "Fierce Fire Makes Ruin of Calistoga" and an account of the disaster:

"Calistoga was almost destroyed by a fire which broke out in the center of the business portion of town at 5:15 this evening ... The flames spread with great rapidity and inside of half an hour had enveloped buildings on both sides. In thirty minutes the flames were communicated to Spiers Livery Stable across the street. The fire department met with a serious handicap by having a line of hose burn. By 7 o'clock the entire business portion of the town and several residences on side streets were a mass of flames or in ruins extending down both sides of Lincoln Avenue for a distance of three blocks, with only five or six buildings remaining on the entire avenue from the wagon bridge to the Southern Pacific depot.

"The principal losers are: D. C. Willis, saloon; H. P. Wilson and Sons, harness shop; J. Wittke, saddler; J. F. Gerber and J. Hiltel, vacant buildings; Mrs. Fred Hall, groceries; F. X. Gravel, shoestore; C. W. Armstrong, drugs; C. A. Carroll, newspaper and printing office; Dr. Fox, dentist; Dr. W. H. Porter, physician; Ed Largey, saloon; the town hall; Magnolia Hotel; G. A. Davis, barber shop; A. Hubbs, notions; Rochdale Company; Bounsall Bros., hardware store and restaurant; Siemsen Bros. and Conner, meat market; William Spiers, livery stable and blacksmith shop; Mrs. Cora Fowle, ice cream parlor; B. F. Grauss, general merchandise; Masonic Hall building; William Conner, residence; Mrs. I. Wixon, millinery; the C. A. Kimball building; the Dr. Gardner building, owned by J. H. Francis; the Harley buildings; C. M. Hoover's grocery; Simmons furniture

59

and undertaker's; Wells Fargo; the Newbauer residence; Badlam's Opera House; the Hubbs building, the Hopper building; and Gilson's jewelry store."

The town gradually rebuilt, only to be hit again by fire in 1907, which burned everything from the railroad tracks to the Grauss building. An exploding oil stove in the George Nance restaurant, formerly the Grauss bakery, was the cause of the fire. The blaze was finally stopped by pulling down the Wells Fargo building.

Like the phoenix, Calistoga came to life again. In recent years, the hot-water area resorts north and west of the railroad tracks have been building up more and more. It is just possible that Sam Brannan's dream of "the best spa in the world" may one day come true.

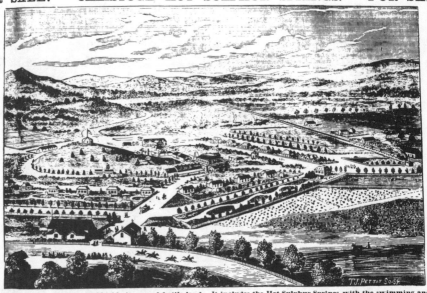

FOR SALE!   CALISTOGA HOT SULPHUR SPRINGS.   FOR SAL

The property consists of 600 acres of highly improved fertile land. It includes the Hot Sulphur Springs, with the swimming and baths; the Hotel and its numerous cottages—37 buildings in all—and 900 village lots, unsold; two large covered water reservoirs; steam-mill site; a fully equipped distillery and refinery, with a cooper shop annexed; 40 acres of bearing grape vines. There is course, and also several miles of carriage drives.

About 1,400 acres of rich adjacent land can also be bought, with two orchards, a vineyard, and 9,000 mulberry trees of choice va adapted to silk culture. The prices of these Estates will be quite moderate, and the terms of payment will be accommodating.

SAMUEL BRANNAN, 420 Montgomery St., San Francis

Bay Area newspaper ad for the sale of Brannan's Hot Springs resort.
Courtesy, Jack Lambrecht

60

The Mines

I T was the backlash of the gold rush to the Mother Lode in the Sierra which started a silver and gold rush to Agua Caliente—or, more accurately, to the hills around and above it.

In 1858-59, prospectors returning from the gold fields started digging in their own hillsides, from Alexander Valley to Calistoga, everywhere they could find a promising outcropping. They were after gold and silver at first and later cinnabar, which is the principal ore used in the production of mercury. Nothing much was found, however, until 1860, when A. J. Bailey and John Cyrus discovered cinnabar on the mountainside facing town. Others prospected successfully over toward Pope Valley, and soon the hillsides were pockmarked with miners' diggings.

The Brannan family also was bitten by the bug. In 1872, Alexander Badlam, son of Mary Ann Brannan, Sam's older sister, staked a claim to the Monitor Ledge, seven miles from Calistoga on the southeast slope of Mount St. Helena, organized the Calistoga Mining Company and opened the Calistoga Gold and Silver Mine, directly behind the Lawley Toll House. The Toll Road having opened for business in 1866, a means of transportation was available for the promoters. Prior to this, Alex and his brother Ezra had long managed Brannan's Hot Springs Hotel.

By 1874, $2,000 in silver bullion per day was being taken out of the mines around Silverado City. During a four-month period, 2,300 tons of ore, reportedly valued at $93,000, were mined.

Badlam built a two-story silver stamp mill on the meadow called Silverado Flat, and a new town sprang up around the diggings. Badlam even laid out streets for his new town, which he christened Silverado City. At one time it was said to number 1,500 souls. A map of the place was actually filed in the office of the county recorder, October 16, 1874, with John Lawley, William Montgomery and William Patterson designated as proprietors.

61

Upper shaft of the Calistoga Gold and Silver mine at Silverado.

"Stevenson at Silverado" by Anne Roller Issler, Robert Louis Stevenson's biographer, contains a sketch of the map of Silverado City, drawn by W. A. Pierce. There were two-hundred and eighty-two lots in thirteen blocks, on streets with names like Fifth Avenue, Gold, Ruby, Silver, Main and Market and covering the whole side of the mountain from below the Toll House inn to the eastern boundary of the mine, some streets running "straight up the mountain."

(Incidentally, the book was out of print for years but has recently been reprinted in paperback by the Napa County Historical Society.)

At Silverado City there were eight businesses, including saloons, the Silverado Hotel, Chapman's boarding house and the Mountain Mill house on the Lake County side. The latter was a stage stop on the way to the mines further up the Lake County road.

The hotel was built in 1874 by Robert L. Thompson and flourished for a year while the mine, which was near the Toll House, was worked extensively. Thompson sold the hotel in 1875 to Sam Chapman, Calistoga mining recorder. It is better known as the "upper boarding house" of Stevenson's "Silverado Squatters."

SILVERADO City was short-lived, however. In late 1875 the Monitor Ledge was cut off by a fault; it has never been re-located. The mine and the town were abandoned. By 1877, all the buildings except the hotel had been torn down or moved away, some to the Grigsby-Palisades Mine lower down the mountainside, northeast of Calistoga. For years miners have prospected all over the mountain range in search of the lost Monitor Ledge; but, as far as is known, it still awaits another discoverer. The Grigsby, the second silver mine discovered locally, was mined off and on until 1941, the last operation by the Palisades Mining Company, which reopened the mine in 1926 with a large crew of men. During the early war years of the 1940s, the price of quicksilver soared because it was difficult to import it from Spain. The price dropped, however, when the tariff was lowered on imports of foreign silver and "quick"; the mine shut down, although some of the buildings are still there. At the height of the mining era, there were sixty-three mines operating in the three-county area surrounding Middletown: twenty-three in Lake County, twenty-eight in Napa, and twelve in Sonoma. In addition to those already mentioned, there were the Mirabel, a name derived from the combination of the proprietors Mills, Randall and Bell, who bought the former Bradford Mine approximately two miles beyond the Lake-Napa County line on the road to Middletown; the Wall Street and Chicago near the Helen Mine; the Abbott and Sulphur Banks; the Napa Consolidated, better known as the Oat Hill Mine, which, with 140,000 flasks, was the biggest producer; Twin Peaks and Corona nearby; Aetna, with 40,000 flasks; the Knoxville, which had the first continuous furnace operation in the United States, designed by the Livermore brothers; the Ida Clayton, one of the first; and the Contact and Socrates on the Sonoma side of the Mayacmas, with the Big Injun and Big Chief nearby. The Socrates was noted for its "free mercury," rich deposits of "liquid ore," which made

63

mining difficult. Miners became salivated from breathing the red dust, causing a loss of teeth and other health problems, a fact which eventually caused the government to step in and close down operations.

Old-timers insist that there is still plenty of high-grade ore in the hills around Calistoga and Middletown. Mine owners say, however, that cost of production is prohibitive.

The bonanza of Oat Hill was an accidental discovery. One day, while dove hunting in the rugged skyline country east of town, William Paul Cook came across an outcropping of cinnabar. He had bent down to pick up a bird when he found the rich ore deposit. Oat Hill was destined to be one of the most productive mines in the Calistoga area. Cook's grandson, by the way, now lives in Porter Creek—Charlie Campbell.

1874 map of Silverado City. —From the Hall of Records, Napa

The Chinese

CHINESE laborers played an important role in the story of mining in California in the latter part of the 1800s. Helen Rocca Goss, who grew up at the Great Western and Helen mines in southern Lake County, gives us a vivid picture of that era in "Life and Death of a Quicksilver Mine." Her father, Andrew Rocca, was superintendent of the Great Western and later owner of the Helen.

The Great Western was one of the most productive in California, recalls Mrs. Goss. All the labor was Chinese, numbering two hundred. Only white men were the foreman, the storekeeper, office employees, technicians and teamsters. Standard wage for Chinese workmen underground in the '90s was $1.25 a day, while that for the ordinary white workmen was $2.26. F. G. McFarling and Andrew Rocca Jr., who were hoist men, received around $100 a month.

Chinese who worked the mines were from the Canton area of China and were two distinct types: the coolies who spoke little or no English and lived in primitive "China camps", and the taller, larger-framed, educated, "superior" men who took care of the coolies and their affairs, collected their pay from the mine bosses and were trusted with the more important underground jobs, such as timbermen, or worked in the stores or as domestics.

Mrs. Goss describes a typical Chinese "coolie camp", which was part of every "quick" mine in Napa, Sonoma and Lake counties:

"The 'China camp' was a mere jumble of huts of the rudest construction, completely lacking in sanitation and surrounded by so much filth and debris that the odors were almost overpowering, even to a passerby. A few of the structures were barracks-like buildings made of rough lumber, but the bulk of the houses was a rambling hodge-podge of shacks built by the men themselves of anything they could lay their hands on— scraps of lumber, old shingles, broken-up packing boxes and flattened-out kerosene cans." Pigs and ducks had freedom of the place.

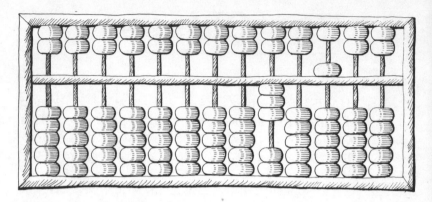

Each man cooked his own rice, heated the water for his tea over a small fire and ate with chopsticks. This was his subsistence.

His usual garb was a kind of dungaree, topped by a large-brimmed, conical, woven-reed hat, his characteristic pigtail hanging down behind.

There were no women in the early camps, wives having been left behind in China. Although every effort was made to keep out prostitutes—because they were a source of dissension among the men—they did appear in camp occasionally, Mrs. Goss recalls, although "we children were always warned not to have anything to do with them."

Every city in Napa County, too, had its "Chinatown", rows of frame buildings connecting with each other and divided by a narrow street or walkway.

In both mines and railroad section-crew camps there was a leader-boss who kept time of the hours each man worked, received all the pay for his men and then paid individual workers in his camp. His calculations were made on an abacus, a source of fascination for old and young whites alike.

L ONG-TIME Calistogans will recall the faithful, devoted Chinese who worked as domestics and gardeners in their homes. These "Chinamen", as they were called, were especially fond of the children in "their" family and never failed to remember birthdays and other occasions with presents and "sweets."

Lelia Crouch, granddaughter of pioneers and a cousin of J. Milton Sherwood, who has returned to the home where she was born after a career with the U. S. Forest Service, has many stories to tell of the Chinese. She still has a beautifully woven, "black-egg" (pickled eggs) basket which had been sent from China. One of the most famous Chinese domestics here, she recalls, was "Old Gow," a six-foot tall "Chinese gentleman," who used to come to town to shop carrying a huge basket. "He was a special favorite of both old and young all over town," she remembers.

When she was a girl, Lelia used to accompany her father, Charlie Crouch, when he would go to read the water meters. She vividly recalls the long row of shacks alongside the ditch beside the railroad tracks across from the SP depot.

"I can still remember the heavy aroma of incense, which seemed to be burning constantly," she says.

Mrs. Goss also recalls the incense. "Every China camp had its josh house, which was a squarish building, used both as a chapel and as a community center. Incense punks were always burning in front of pictures of Chinese rulers or gods."

Different from mine coolies, the Chinese who lived across the railroad tracks in Calistoga worked as section crews and had houses built by the railroad, with long overhanging porches to shade the afternoon sun. Life of section-crew Chinese was not as harsh as that of the mine coolies.

There were about 375,000 Chinese in the United States by 1880, encouraged by a U.S.-China treaty pushing their immigration. Most of these settled in California, where they were welcomed by both mine and railroad owners, who badly needed unskilled workers.

The largest concentration of Chinese in the mines was at Oathill Mine, where they at one time numbered 2,500, and at Aetna Mine in Pope Valley, with 1,200.

Because the Chinese were not allowed to stake mining claims, however, many left the mines and went into other occupations. Were it not for the Chinese, the big supply of labor for the "empire builders", the great railroad joining the East and West probably may not have been built—or as soon. They were builders of dams and stone bridges and picturesque stone fences, many of which can be seen today all over the valley. They hewed out the long underground limestone tunnels at Schramsberg, Beringer's and other wineries; and, in addition to being faithful domestics, gardeners and laundrymen, they were also successful businessmen, as well as laborers in vineyards and orchards, especially after the Indians left.

One of the principal businesses in early Calistoga was Kong Sam Kee's laundry and employment office, opened in 1875

on Lincoln Avenue. "RLS" has made him famous through the pages of the "Squatters."

Y ET the Chinese went mostly unappreciated, considered "heathen" by their neighbors, who did not understand them and their close-knit family ways. Fred Hutchinson, whose father, Thomas Brannan Hutchinson, once ran a grocery store in Calistoga and went on to become county district attorney, tells of the long-suffering Chinese he knew as a boy in Napa and Calistoga. ("T. B. Hutchinson" by Fred Hutchinson, published in 1950.)

"Chinese workers were constantly annoyed by the children of the town, who were afraid of them," he writes. "There was a deep ditch running along Lincoln from the Springs Ground to the river, and the Chinese had constructed flimsy board bridges across it. On occasions when the ditch was full of water, the kids of the town would remove the boards and throw rocks at the laundry. The Chinese would open the door and come tumbling down into the water."

Agitation against the hard-working, conscientious Orientals was started by white laborers as early as the 1850s. The picture worsened as jobs for workers grew scarce after completion of the Transcontinental Railroad in 1869. Many white settlers felt that the Chinese were taking jobs which rightly belonged to white persons.

Since the mines depended almost exclusively on Chinese for underground labor, mine owners were up in arms over what they called "unfairness of the law to the corporations of California." They were joined by the railroads, which also needed Chinese labor; and the Orientals were allowed to remain.

Not for long, however. In 1882 Congress passed the Chinese Exclusion Act, which forbade Asiatics to enter the United States.

"The Chinese must go" campaign in California caused especial bitterness. In fact, the state legislature had begun passing discriminatory legislation against the "Chinamen" in 1852; and the state Constitution adopted in 1879 required the legislature to set up the "conditions governing the residence of objectionable persons." One law subsequently passed prohibited corporations with state charters from employing "any Chinese or Mongolian", establishing heavy penalties for violations. (*Alta California*, March 23, 1880.)

And so the Chinese eventually passed from the local scene, except for domestics in wealthy valley families.

In Calistoga, along with most of the business section of the town, Chinatown was wiped out in the disastrous fire of August 2, 1901.

It wasn't too long, however, before Calistoga — and Chinatown — was rebuilt, the entire community, including the Chinese, pitching in to help.

Stage Coaches and Road Agents

A vital link in the history of Napa, Sonoma and Lake counties was the stagecoach-freight wagon driver. Except for the horse and "shank's mare," there was just no other way to bridge the vast distances between Vallejo and Suscol on the south to the Hot Springs, to the Big Geysers, the mines and on up to Clear Lake or to Healdsburg and Cloverdale.

Horse-drawn passenger and freight traffic was the lifeblood of the burgeoning area, especially during the heyday of the mines and the spas in Lake and Napa counties, where resorts were numerous. From 1857, when William Fisher came to Napa to serve as agent for Nathan Coombs daily stage line between Napa and Benicia, on through the 1880s and 1890s, stage-coach lines criss-crossed the landscape of Lake County, over into Sonoma, down into Napa and on to Solano, where connections were made with steamers from San Francisco, Stockton and Sacramento. It was not until 1910 that the stage-coach gave way to the motorbus.

Horse-drawn passenger and freight vehicles used four or six horses, though freighters themselves preferred the "four-in-hand" canvas-covered all-purpose wagon. Passenger coaches were usually drawn by six or eight horses, and the stagecoaches themselves were of the thoroughbrace "Concord" type; that is, the body was suspended on leather straps for greater riding comfort. Smaller two-or three-seated rigs were used for less-traveled roads.

When the Napa Valley Railroad was completed to Oak Knoll, Fisher moved from Napa to become express manager for the Pacific Union Express Company; and when Wells Fargo bought out Pacific Union, Fisher decided to start a stage business of his own between Calistoga and Healdsburg. He sold his interests in that line when the North Pacific Railroad was built and devoted his time to the Lodi Stables in Calistoga, operating the Clear Lake and Calistoga Stage Line.

CLEAR LAKE AND CALISTOGA STAGE LINE,

CARRYING U. S. MAIL, AND WELLS, FARGO & CO.'S EXPRESS.

1882---SUMMER ARRANGEMENT---1882

SAN FRANCISCO to LAKEPORT in ELEVEN HOURS.

Passengers leave San Francisco daily by Ferry from Market St. Wharf, at 8:00 a. m., arriving in Calistoga at 11:15 a. m.

COACHES LEAVE CALISTOGA DAILY [SUNDAYS EXCEPTED] AT

☞ On Tuesdays, Thursdays and Saturdays ☜

Leave Calistoga for LAKEPORT, via MIDDLETOWN, GLENBROOK, KELSEYVILLE and SODA BAY, returning alternate days.

THIS IS THE MOST DIRECT LINE FROM SAN FRANCISCO TO LAKEPORT,

and the most picturesque and romantic route on the Coast. From Mt. St. Helena it affords the traveler a beautiful view of the far famed Napa and Russian River Valleys and mountains of the Coast Range; and from Cobb Mountain the great Clear Lake region in front and the Pacific in the distance. This line connects with stages for ADAMS, SEIGLER and HOWARD SPRINGS and SODA BAY.

☞ On Mondays, Wednesdays and Fridays ☜

Stages leave Calistoga at 12 m. for MIDDLETOWN, GUENOC, LOWER LAKE and SUL-PHUR BANK, returning alternate days. This line connects at Lower Lake with stages for Seigler, Howard, Adams and the celebrated BARTLETT SPRINGS.

THESE LINES ARE STOCKED WITH SIX-HORSE CONCORD COACHES,

And handled by the most careful and experienced drivers.

TICKETS FOR SALE in Lakeport, at W. W. Greene's Hotel, John Clark, Agent; Kelsey-ville, at Wells, Fargo & Co.'s Office, A. A. Slocum, Agent; at C. P. R. R. Office, Market St. Wharf, also at No. 2 New Montgomery Street, San Francisco, Samuel Miller, Agent.

ROUND TRIP TICKETS, From Lakeport to San Francisco and return, TWELVE DOLLARS.

SINGLE TRIP TICKETS, - - - - - $6.50.

W. F. FISHER, Proprietor, Calistoga, Cal.

Courtesy, Pete Molinari

Fisher became an important figure in the business and civic life of Calistoga. He developed the Calistoga Water Company, building a reservoir in Feige Canyon west of town, and for years served the community with water, until the town bought out the Fisher Water Works in 1918 for $40,000. Feige Canyon wells still supply Calistoga with water, in addition to the Kimball Reservoir on Mount St. Helena above town.

In 1873 Fisher married Agnes M. Safley and built a big house on Main Street. One of their three children, Alice, was the mother of Larry Armstrong of Cloverleaf Ranch, Santa Rosa. The C. C. Simics now own the Fisher house.

ANOTHER early reinsman was Clark "Old Chieftain" Foss, a native of New Hampshire. Skillful and daring, he drove the first "coach and six" to the Big Geysers in Sonoma County by way of the old road through Alexander Valley to Healdsburg in 1863.

Clark Foss. —*Courtesy, Pete Molinari*

With travel to the famed resort increasing, Foss built a shorter road to The Geysers, through Knight's Valley and up what is now known as the Briggs-Lamoreaux road, charging passengers one dollar per mile. The tortuous road was, in many places, a seven-foot shelf clinging to the mountainside, with drops of hundreds of feet to picturesque valleys far below and sharp curves more the rule than the exception.

That there weren't more accidents and collisions was a tribute to Foss' and other drivers' expertise in handling the reins.

THE *Independent Calistogian* reported in 1879 that Foss "drove his six-in-hand as though four fiends were after him, directing them by his thundering voice as much as with his huge fists, and at the same time snapping his long whip with a shot like a pistol, echoing through the hills."

On the level his voice would thunder "Shake! Shake! Shake One!", and the well-trained team would fly over the road.

When Foss said, "Down!", they slowed to a steady trot. "Way down!", to a dead stop, "Shake!", and they were off again.

More people came to ride behind the redoubtable Foss over the Hog's Back, over the "ridgepole of the world", than came to see The Geysers, "bumping, bouncing over stones and ruts, swaying from side to side", according to Mrs. Issler.

A younger and equally daring stage driver, Bill Spiers, spoke often of Foss' skill with the reins.

"Colonel Foss," he told Mrs. Issler when she was here researching for her RLS stories, "could handle six horses like you'd handle that many cats. He would lift them right off their feet and swing them around corners so fast you couldn't see the lead team. He drove his stage to the Big Geysers for years, and he'd run down the last hill with a yell to wake the dead."

The register of guests who came and went at Foss House, the hotel at Fossville, which was the half-way stop between Calistoga and the Big Geysers, at the entrance of Knight's Valley, has been preserved and is now in the possession of the George Turner family of Calistoga.

One day recently I had the privilege of going through the book, which bears the signatures of many famous persons. In fact, it was thrilling to see names such as H.S. Crocker, Ulysses S. Grant, Jacob Schram, Commodore John Rodgers, Joseph M. Strong, who was Robert Louis Stevenson's stepson-in-law and the artist who sketched the original of the frontispiece of "Stevenson at Silverado," James Flood, Mark Hopkins, bankers J. Pierpont Morgan and G. L. Chase, W.R. Hearst, A.L. Tubbs, Sr., and also Sam Brannan and his relatives, the Winans and Badlam families, and pages and pages of others, many with flowery comments about stage-driver Foss and who-ever was the cook—both good, they said.

Unfortunately, Frieda Turner told me, someone has excised the signature of Robert Louis Stevenson, which was also believed there at one time.

Like many descendants of early upvalley families, several Turners still live here, including Tom, Henry, and their late brother Frank's widow, Lena; and Frank's sons, Frank Jr. and George, and their families. Grandmother Maggie Turner, who was a child when Robert Louis Stevenson lived here, knew the author well; he used to visit her parents, the Frank McDonalds, who became hosts at Foss House when the Colonel moved his business to Calistoga. Maggie's two other sons, Walter and the late Gordon Turner, went into business elsewhere.

Because Foss served many mines, he was constantly harassed by highwaymen and developed great skill and daring in eluding them. Ironically, he was killed in a wreck when his horses ran away with his coach.

There were many other stage and freight drivers, including Clarence Myers, Bill and Joe Downey, Will Carter, Jerdon and Newt Connor, Allen Palmer, Fred Higgins, H. T. "Tuck" Quigley, E. B. Stoddard and Johnny Gardiner. It was Gardiner who helped bring the notorious highwayman Buck English to justice.

$\mathcal{B}$UT, of the many skilled reinsmen who piloted their teams through the hills and valleys of Lake and Napa counties, the man most closely tied in with the history of both areas and the man who was foremost in opening up Lake County to development was Bill "Finest Kind!" Spiers.

A native of Kentucky, where he was born August 29, 1853, Spiers rose from woodcutter to quicksilver miner to freight-wagon driver and eventually to operator of his own stage line as well as canny businessman and Calistoga civic leader, a typical "self-made man" in the best tradition of the American West and its early "modern-day" transition from the late 1880s on into the first quarter of the twentieth century.

"Finest Kind!" he was known as; and Bill Spiers liked the nickname. He acquired it from his well-known reply to all questions, whether about his health, the weather, the state of the nation, his community or the world in general: "Finest kind!"

Young Bill Spiers grew up on his parents' 4,000-acre farm in Kentucky and went with them at the age of fourteen to Missouri. Like many young men of that time, he caught the "Go West, young man!" fever and left his family to travel to the West Coast in 1872. He worked first as a woodcutter in Napa and later at a quicksilver mine near Pine Flat in Sonoma County, reportedly earning $1,040 at the diggings. He was to save this sum and use it later on to set himself up in business in Calistoga. He came here in 1876 to haul freight to the Great Western, Oat Hill and other mines.

"During the summer Louis Stevenson spent in this country," writes Anne Roller Issler, "Bill Spiers was hauling bark to a Napa tannery. He had eight mules and a 'back-action' and hauled eleven cords at one time. Sometimes, when he wasn't hauling bark, he drove a rig for William F. Fisher, owner of the Calistoga livery barn."

Bill came to know young Stevenson well.

"I drove him up the mountain more than once!", Spiers told Mrs. Issler. "I didn't know he'd be so famous, or I'd have noticed him more particular. I drove him up to Silverado in a four-horse rig one hot day, trottin' the horses all the way so they was in an awful sweat when we got there; and I says to him, 'What the hell's your hurry?' Didn't seem to me he had so much

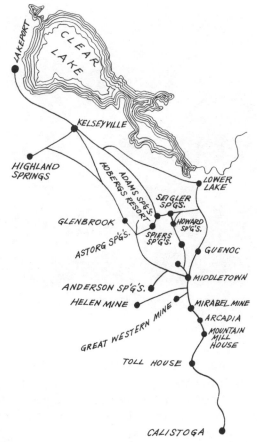

Spiers' stage route to Lake County resorts.

to do that we had to race up the mountain. Fact is, I thought him kind of a fool, livin' in that old shack writin' books! I was a few years younger than he was, but I didn't think he was hardly as smart as I which had got my diplomy back in Kentucky when I was seven and a half."

Bill had a good head for business. With the money he had saved, he bought the stage line from Calistoga to towns and resorts in Lake County and soon controlled all connecting lines. For freight he used cumbersome wagons whose lead horses usually wore hame bells, so-called because they were attached to the hames, which carried the lines on each side of the horse collar. The sound of the approaching vehicles and tinkling bells could be heard not only through miles and miles of canyon roads but also in town, so that everyone knew when to expect them at the Magnolia Hotel stage office.

Spiers' stage in front of Magnolia Hotel. Courtesy, Ella Rush Spiers

IT must have been a lively time in front of the hotel every time the stages came in, five or six a day, some with as many as eight horses. Passengers and baggage and townspeople and small boys and dogs—the town came to life with the excitement of the stage-coach arrival.

Long-time Calistogans well remember seeing Mattie Spiers, standing in front of the Magnolia, meeting each stage.

"She always wore a big leather bag in front of her, wide open at the top, and she sold tickets for the stages out of it," one old-timer told me.

Spiers had married Martha J. Simpson of Grove City, Pennsylvania, a school-teacher, in 1881. It was she who always attended to the business side of things. The couple had three children—James, Mary and Alden, the latter better known as "Buck." Ella Rush Spiers, "Buck's" widow, lives in Calistoga. She told me her father, Charles Rush, worked for Spiers, repairing stages, making frames for the coaches, shoeing horses and building bodies for motorized stages. Of him, Louis Vermeil of the Owl Garage here, who himself is an expert with automobiles and other machinery, says, "Rush was a genius with anything mechanical!" Louis still uses some of Rush's tools.

Although freights and stages practically had the old Toll Road to themselves over Mount St. Helena, whenever one of the new "gasoline wagons" did come along, reinsmen had to exert every skill to keep their vehicles right-side up because their horses were frightened.

Lois Carroll Winston, until a few years ago editor and publisher of *The Weekly Calistogan*, wrote a colorful series of "Do You Remember?" stories for the centennial edition of the paper in 1959. She says that "Bill Spiers once told Mr. Livermore, who owned a pretentious summer home on the Lake County side of the mountain, that he would shoot Livermore if the latter insisted on driving his automobile over the Toll Road."

However, with the introduction of more and more automobiles, Spiers, always keeping abreast of the times, supplemented his horse-drawn vehicles with new motorbuses; and eventually, in the three-year period between 1912 and 1915, he completely converted his whole fleet to motorized equipment.

BILL often told of his drivers' being robbed on the way to or from the mines, the expressbox containing payrolls or bullion from the many mines being the attraction.

It was not until 1910 that the drivers gave up carrying shotguns; but no matter how brave, ingenious or colorful the reinsmen were, more often than not the highwaymen made off among the mountain crags and dense under-brush with not only the express box but also passengers' valuables.

Spiers monopolized passenger trade over the Toll Road and also had government contracts to carry the mail. No one could ever be sure that the stages would not be held up, not only before the 1880s, the gold-mining days, but also into the quick-silver mining period that followed.

It became commonplace for articles in *The Calistogian*, The Napa *Register*, The San Francisco *Chronicle* and *Examiner*, Oakland *Tribune* and other newspapers to report regularly on activities of the highwaymen.

"Black Bart" and Tom Bell were two robbers of the earlier days, who seemed to have an "itch" to write poems or notes to officers of the law; later highwaymen seemed to specialize in being on such intimate terms with their victims or the passersby that they called them by their first names and tried to send messages by them to mutual friends, according to Mrs. Goss. ("Highwaymen in the Quicksilver Mining Region," a quarterly of the Historical Society of Southern California, September, 1955.)

Waylaying the stage was so prevalent that Andrew Rocca often preferred, his daughter says, to ride his saddle horse to Calistoga himself to bring back money for his mine employees. At times he would vary his route since there were, fortunately, two ways to get to and from Napa Valley: one via the fourteen-mile Lawley Toll Road over the mountain and then up the two-mile stretch of mine road; or the other longer and much steeper way, and therefore not so much used, the Ida Clayton. Her father often eluded robbers by taking the latter route, says Mrs. Goss.

In the mid-80s Rocca and a partner opened a drug store in Middletown and put in a Wells Fargo agency. After that, Bill Spiers' stage brought in the mines' payroll, with an armed messenger riding topside beside the driver.

Considering the danger of robbery along the stage routes, it is surprising that so little precaution was made when loading the express box. Mrs. Goss tells how "the messenger and helper would come to the stage, lugging the heavy box, grunting and puffing to advertise to the world what a back-breaking load they were carrying. The box was locked, of course, but the bandits simply shot off the lock when they did get it, anyway. It would have been quite easy for a man on horseback to get out of town ahead of the stage and lie in wait for it. And that, apparently, was what generally did happen when the stage was held up."

Robberies were so common in gold, silver and "quick"

regions that newspapers took to identifying dates of events with "on the day the stage was robbed"; or "the stage was robbed again today at the usual place."

Highwaymen's costumes ranged from that of the "Lone Highwayman" described in *The Calistogian* for June 27, 1888: a flour-sack mask, an old black hat, blue overalls over black pantaloons, and a light denim shirt and carrying a Winchester"; to "Black Bart"'s linen duster, flour-sack mask and shotgun.

"Black Bart," identified after capture as Charles E. Boles, operated mostly in the Sonora gold-mining country and had a record of holding up twenty-eight stages in six years; but he was also known to visit Napa County frequently.

Many robbers were in reality friends and neighbors who engaged in robbing out of need or for the fun of it and even called the driver or occupants of the stage by name—"Ed, when you get back to Kelseyville, give the boys my regards!" Others, however, were the real thing.

"Black Bart" was the former type; Buck English was the latter. Bart said he never used his gun, even said it had never been loaded. A laundry mark on a handkerchief lost during his one unsuccessful holdup in 1883 led to his arrest by a Wells Fargo detective at his rooming house in San Francisco.

BUCK English was another sort. Newspapers of the time variously describe him as "a master highwayman, a swashbuckling desperado who stole cattle and horses and robbed helpless pedestrians as well as stages"; a "gentleman highwayman" from a prominent Lake County family; and even as "the youngest of six brothers of a desperado father, all of whom lived violently. All served terms in prison and several met death as violently as they had lived."

The last escapade of the English gang was in May, 1895. A. R. Palmer was driving stage for Spiers that day. The San Francisco *Examiner* for May 8, said:

"The highwaymen went about their work like old hands, one in particular as cool as if he was collecting taxes. His voice was deep and brusk as he ordered, 'Throw down the box!' He was about five feet, eleven, and, like the others, wore a mask and was nearly covered by a dark grey duster, his overalls and old shoes showing beneath, and a black slouch hat. Both were armed with old-style Colt revolvers and cursed and swore at everyone, especially the Chinese, who was knocked down and badly beaten."

Bill Spiers.
Courtesy, Ella Rush Spiers

It was this last item—a hatred for Chinese—which eventually led to Buck's identification. He was often quoted with a remark in a saloon like, "Well, it's getting to be about time to meet some more Chinamen on the trail."

This particular day, while the robbery was going on, two freight wagons from Middletown came along, one driven by Byrd Hunt.

"How are you, Byrd?", Buck is reported to have said, jocularly, as the bandits took off in the direction of Oat Hill Mine.

Pretty much fed up with such incidents by this time, authorities organized a posse, which included Under Sheriff Robert Brownlee, Theodore A. Bell, the young and promising district attorney of Napa County, John Williams, and J.N. True. The four came upon the robbers, who by this time were on the down-stage from Monticello, on the Napa side of Berryessa Valley. After a wild shoot-out chase, with "level-headed behavior" on the part of the driver, Johnny Gardiner, English was badly wounded, and the robbers were captured. English spent most of the rest of his life in jail.

The leading role Bell played in the arrest and conviction of English helped spearhead his political career. He went on to serve as Congressman and to be nominated for governor of California in 1906 and 1910.

After this well-publicized incident, Spiers and his stage drivers breathed a little more freely.

NOT only was "Finest kind!" an astute businessman; he was also a progressive citizen of his community. Realizing the potential which lay in the hot under-ground mineral springs beneath the Calistoga township, he at one time considered leasing the Hot Springs and erected an imposing redwood gate at the entrance. It was Spiers who operated the town's first successful electric plant, having taken over the W. H. Pitman set of generators and gas engines on the creek below the old flour mill, hiring Fred Popp as manager. Spiers strung wires across Lincoln Avenue, dangling four-hundred light bulbs from them. He later sold the plant to Snow Mountain Power and Light Company, which in turn sold to PG&E.

In another venture, Spiers converted the former clay-processing plant at First and Washington to a stage barn and garage. Incidentally, that kaolin clay was mined up Teale Canyon and, after processing was sent to San Francisco to be made into tableware. Spiers sold the building to Charles Piner, who tore it down when he built his spa.

Spiers served as town councilman for thirty-six years and as mayor many times, as well as being active in civic and fraternal organizations. He also owned the town hearse but was never known to have charged the poor for service. Like many other businesses, his place was destroyed by the big fire in 1901; but he rebuilt, farther up the street, about where the Bank of America now is located. (Spiers' later stables also burned down, in 1952.)

Just before his death in April, 1931, Bill was planning to expand operations northward, having bought the Oregon, Idaho and California Stage Company.

Were it not for Spiers and his stages, the fabulous era of the Lake County mineral springs resorts would not have been possible, according to Ella Spiers. "Bill opened up the whole southern end of the county for development and prosperity," she told me.

One need only look at a map of the resort area in southern Lake County to see how influential "Finest Kind" had been in helping to keep not only the spas but also the mines going concerns. Stages and freight wagons stopped first at Mount St. Helena Inn (the former Toll House); then on to Mountain Mill House a short distance down the grade; on to Mirabel Mine and Middletown, Spring Hill Farm, Harbin Springs, Anderson Springs, Mira Vista, Spiers Springs, Adams and Seigler Springs, Bonanza and Howard Springs, Hoberg's, Glenbrook and Salmina, Lower Lake, McIntire Ranch, Kelseyville, and on to Lakeport, the final stop before turning back home to Calistoga.

MANY were the stories of the latter-day Bill Spiers and his big automobiles, which he drove around town at about ten to fifteen miles an hour. One day, while autos were still a novelty, he steered one of his first cars right into a flagpole which stood in the center of the principal intersection of town, at Washington and Lincoln, putting about $300-worth of dents in the car but not damaging the flagpole much.

"In those days," Mrs. Winston recalls in her column "Do You Remember?", "Spiers could drive six horses better than a car; but he later became expert with motorized vehicles."

In fact, Bill was to meet his death doing just what he had done most of his life—in the driver's seat. One day he was slowly driving down Washington near what is now the firehouse when he suffered a fatal heart attack.

The Calistogan for April 10, 1931, carried the following story of what happened:

"Shortly after turning the corner off Lincoln Avenue, going toward the electric depot, he was overcome by a stroke, but not until after he realized something was wrong; for he had thrown his car out of gear, turned off the switch, and had his foot on the brake but probably did not have enough remaining strength to absolutely bring the big Lincoln to a complete standstill. The car rolled along at about five miles an hour until it struck a pillar supporting the awning of the electric station. Fortunately, he did not run into anybody, and no one was hurt."

The town he served so well remembers Bill Spiers. A special feature of the new Pioneer Museum is devoted to him and his achievements.

Lawley and the Old Toll Road

CALISTOGA almost became the locale of yet another landmark—or, rather, Mount St. Helena did; and James Lick, American financier-philanthropist and friend of both Sam Brannan and Leland Stanford, was involved in this deal, too.

Just as he had nixxed Stanford's plan for a university on the Springs Ground, Lick, because of a quarrel with John Lawley, turned the final selection of his Lick Observatory to Mount Hamilton in Santa Clara County.

Details of the quarrel with Lawley, founder of the Toll Road over the mountain, were never learned; but an early newspaper account says that Mount St. Helena had been preferred as a site for the observatory because it had the "greatest number of clear days and it was taller than Mount Hamilton."

Lawley had been given a government permit March 17, 1866, to establish his toll road on the strength of the announcement that a railroad was coming to Calistoga. An experienced banker, he based his conclusions of the toll road's success on the fact that traffic was becoming steady up and over the mountain into Lake County, especially after the mines became more numerous and productive.

Lawley was a Southerner, born in Alabama. He had taught school and also superintended work in mills and plantations before coming to California. In 1854 he established the Banner Warehouse in Napa and sometime later purchased a portion of the Jose Berryessa land grant in Berryessa Valley. In 1877 he moved on to Pope Valley to engage in quicksilver mining at the Phoenix Mine, turning over operation of the Toll House Inn and road to his son, "Uncle Charley", and daughter, Mollie.

If the Lawleys weren't appreciated by James Lick, they certainly were by their Mount St. Helena neighbors, including the famed hunter "100-bucks-a-year" Rufe Hansen of "Silverado Squatters" fame.

Mrs. Issler says that "Uncle Charley", like Stevenson, must have been "somewhat of a poet." Both men had seen and marveled at the sea fogs which blocked out the valley at times, covering all but the highest peaks. She quotes Charley Lawley's description of the fog, which Stevenson devotees will enjoy comparing with the latter's:

"At daybreak," he said, "the fog lies perfectly quiet, like water in a calm. When the sun comes out, it begins to move and climb. Mountain peaks and hills are islands until the fog moves higher and blots them out. Napa Valley on the east and Sonoma Valley to the west at last fill up, and all of the islands are gone. And then, if you climb higher up the mountain, you look out over rolling billows. The hotter the sun, the more motion in the fog, you know. On a very bright day, the peak of Mount Saint Helena is reflected as though in a sea. Before such sights an old man like me takes off his hat."

THREE deer hunters of my acquaintance had a similar, even more awe-inspiring experience.

"It was just before sunup," Arch, my husband, told me. "We were sitting under the huge boulders overlooking the first switchback on the mountain, waiting for daylight—Harry Patten, Cyril Saviez and I. The fog lay five-hundred yards below us, with only the tops of the hills visible above it, looking for all the world like giant battleships. It was very still and peaceful.

"Suddenly, off to the right below us, a huge mushroom of a cloud ballooned up out of the fog, just like an atomic bomb, and sat there! It was the eeriest sight I'd ever seen! And then it roiled and cascaded and boiled up again, just like somebody below was throwing it back up every time it tried to fall back!"

The three hunters stared, fascinated, nobody saying a word at fiirst.

It was Arch who finally broke the silence. "WHAT in the hell is that?"

Harry Patten, whose whole life had been lived on the mountain, chuckled a little and then explained, "THAT'S the old Faithful Geyser down on Tubbs Lane!"

The trio watched until the roiling and billowing ceased, and the geyser collapsed. Arch and Cy haven't been up there at

"Old Faithful" erupting above the sea fogs.

exactly the same moment and circumstances since when Old Faithful erupted of a foggy morning. However, both say that the sight is so spectacular that it is well worth the climb and the wait.

ALSO worth the drive, with its panoramic view of King's Canyon and the High Rocks, is the Old Toll Road, which leaves Lake County Highway two miles northeast of Calistoga, winds its way along the foothills for a while, and then turns abruptly at Radelfinger ranch, crosses over a creek (possifly the one into which James Lick was summarily dumped), to edge along the cliffsides and on up toward the pass to join the new roadway short of the nick which marks the division of the Mayacmas range. The macadam road cuts through the old route in many places, and John Lawley's road joins the modern highway short of Hanly's.

It was on the flat below the steep rise of mountain wall just beyond the pass that Lawley built his Toll House Inn, with a swinging pole gate across the road for collection of fees. That bar was a long beam which turned on a post and was kept horizontal by a counterweight of stones. At sundown it was tied to a tree on the farther side.

When the original inn burned down, the Silverado

Lawley Toll House and toll gate.

House nearby was moved to the site. It eventually collapsed under the weight of heavy snow in 1948.

For years the board sign on which was written a schedule of fees for passage through the toll gate hung in the city hall on Washington Street: one-horse rig, 50 cents; two-horse team and wagon, 75 cents; four-horse stage, $1; six-horse stage, $1.25; eight-horse stage, $1.50. The toll board is the property of Frank Piner, former manager of the local Bank of America, and is presently on loan to the Stevenson Museum in St. Helena.

Mollie F. (Lawley) Patten succeeded her brother Charley in the operation of the inn and toll gate. One of the first graduates of what is now Mills College, she also became one of the state's outstanding personalities, a friend of the many famous persons who came and went over the mountain. Her husband Dan was superintendent of the Phoenix Mine, which was over toward the High Rocks and down toward Aetna Springs.

MOLLIE'S son, Harry Patten, mining engineer and life-long prospector, spent years digging in the hills above

and around town, always hoping to re-discover the lost Monitor

LAWLEY TOLL ROAD
MAIN THOROFARE TO
LAKE CO. FROM 1868 to 1922
RATES of TOLL

	SINGLE TRIP	ROUND TRIP
1 HORSE RIG	.50	1.00
2 HORSE TEAM & WAGON	.75	1.00
4 HORSE TEAM & WAGON	1.00	2.00
6 HORSE TEAM & WAGON	1.25	2.50
8 HORSE TEAM & WAGON	1.50	3.00
SADDLE HORSE	.10	.20
LOOSE HORSES & CATTLE	.10	.20
HOGS, SHEEP & GOATS	.03	
MOTOR CYCLE	.25	.50

AUTOS

	SINGLE TRIP	ROUND TRIP
2 PASSENGER CARS OR UNDER	.75	1.00
OVER 2 AND NOT EXCEEDING 5 PASSENGERS	1.00	1.50
OVER 5 NOT EXCEEDING 7 PASSENGER CAPACITY CAR	1.25	2.00
ALL OVER 7 PASSENGER CAPACITY CAR	1.50	2.50

TRUCKS

	SINGLE TRIP	ROUND TRIP
1 TON TRUCK	.85	1.30
2 TON TRUCK	1.00	2.50
3 TON TRUCK	1.25	1.75
4 TON TRUCK	1.50	2.25
5 TON TRUCK	1.75	2.50
7 TON TRUCK	2.50	5.00
TRACTORS	2.50	

Lawley toll-rate board, now in the Silverado Museum,
courtesy of Mr. and Mrs. Frank Piner.

Ledge or even another, richer deposit. It was he who, in the dark depression days of the 1930s, undertook the gargantuan task of building the twisting, switch-backing road up the south and east side of Mount St. Helena to the top of the fourth peak, highest point of the Mayacmas.

"They" said he couldn't do it, that it was a foolhardy, impossible task.

"Just give me enough CCC's and TED TAMAGNI (he emphasized the name), and we'll get the job done!", Harry told the Doubting Thomases.

The road, still in excellent shape today and traversed by some of the biggest equipment you wouldn't believe WAS built, a prodigious achievement and manifest testimony to the genius and grit of those who worked on it. Tamagni, who was one of the best bulldozer operators in the business, narrowly escaped death several times when his 'dozer rolled off the near perpendicular cliff. I've been up that spectacular road, all the way to the forestry lookout station at the top; I'll be the first to admit that it takes a lot of nerve to look down that sheer drop of

Aerial view of Bear and Cub Valley.   Photo by Ted Miller

hundreds of feet, even though the scenery is magnificent. The road itself is clearly visible from town, its long stretches and switchbacks outlined against the dark mountainside, its tortuous path hacked out of sheer rock and stubborn lava by Harry, Ted and the unnamed boys of the Civilian Conservation Corps.

It was Harry and Ted and other intrepid buck hunters and prospectors who, as far as it is known, first gainsaid the long-held opinion that Mount St. Helena was once a volcano. Not so, they countered, pointing toward the deep, rugged valley which lies behind the Palisades and stretches from Cathedral Rock to Swartz Canyon.

Not exactly a Doubting Thomas myself but curious to see the "real crater," I asked Arch to drive me up that zigzag dirt road to Pigeon Point, the most southeasterly switchback on No. One Peak, where we could look directly across to the back side of the High Rocks and down into Bear and Cub Valley.

Sure enough, the scraggy dark-gray-and-brown rocks and hardened basalt "froth" which make up the floor of the crater and abundance of metamorphic masses rimming the entire valley without doubt resemble a volcanic arena. In the center and sunk deep into the hardened agglomerate is a dark, cone-like peak; and off to the southeast rises a high mountain hunters call Sugarloaf. It would be interesting to hear what geologists and other experts think about Bear and Cub Valley's being the real crater, rather than the sawed-off top of the nearby mountain, as some believe.

"We have walked through this crater many times, following a buck," Arch told me, "and it sure is tough on shoe leather —dark and flinty and like hardened sponge."

Stevenson mentions that Silverado was within "walking distance" of Oat Hill, the former stage-stop town beyond Sugarloaf and past Maple Springs, right at the pass over the High Rocks. If RLS walked there, he must have gone via Bear and Cub Valley, the shortest route! Quite a walk, whichever way one looks at it! Not much is left of Oat Hill, by the way—only a mine shaft and some foundation stones, ruins of what once was the Halfway House.

At any rate, Stevenson loved this country, which is perhaps why he selected the locale of Mount St. Helena and the stark beauty of Cathedral Rock and the Palisades as his setting for some of "Treasure Island" action.

Lillie Hitchcock Coit in her favorite fireman's costume. From a family portrait

Firebelle Lillie

THE name of Lillie Hitchcock Coit should not be glossed over with a mere mention. For, if Sam Brannan was the most fascinating man Calistoga had ever known, then surely the witty and dashing Lillie would qualify as the woman who stood out as "the very essence of the new frontier that was California," according to Helen Holdredge in "Firebelle Lillie", a biography of the Southern family which was well-known in San Francisco social circles during the period when the war between the states was dividing the country.

Lillie was already famous for her "sheer joy of being alive and sharing that joy with all those who knew her" before the family transferred from the South to the Army post in San Francisco, where her father was to serve as Medical Director for the West Coast.

Dr. Hitchcock bought acreage from Louis Bruck in Napa Valley, including much of what is now Bothe-Napa Valley State Park and across the fields toward the Silverado Trail. The tall, dark-haired Lillie spent a great deal of time at Lonely, as her parents called the estate in the canyon known today as Drake's Grove, partying and driving about the countryside in short skirt and boots in her four-horse "tally-ho" coach. She would ride from Lonely to the White Sulphur Springs Hotel west of St. Helena, always with several young men in tow, says Mrs. Holdredge, "for Lillie was always popular, and merrymaking was her main object in life."

An honorary member of Knickerbocker Number Five Engine Company in San Francisco, Lillie always proudly wore the fireman's badge the department had given her. In fact, she had a uniform made in Paris similar to that worn by the firemen, complete with official badge.

"Miss Lil" and "Number Five's Sweetheart" she was fondly and admiringly called, even by envious firemen of other companies. She liked to sit "up front" with the driver, playing her banjo or guitar as the men sang chanteys. It was the custom, Mrs. Holdredge says, for the firemen to sing when fighting fires because the rhythmic chant seemed to allay the anxiety of fire victims.

Lillie's friends included Mark Twain, Cincinnatus (Joaquin) Miller, Ambrose Bierce, Robert Louis Stevenson and Clark Foss who, along with Bill Spiers, was making stagecoach driving history in northern California. It was Foss who taught the dashing Lillie to drive, even to handle six horses' lines.

It was said of her that she "drove like a cavalry officer and played poker like one, even drank bourbon and smoked cigars on occasion," while at the same time managing to be the complete lady, admired and respected by all who knew her.

Even after her marriage to Howard Coit, Dr. Hitchcock could deny his daughter nothing. He built for her a splendid house three miles from Lonely out in the vineyards of mid-valley —a Hindu bungalow, painted dark brown and rambling, in the form of a Maltese cross, with glass doors on all sides opening to porches and a dining-room extension in back. A large patio in the center of the house was roofed over with glass; and the house itself was beautifully furnished with a piano, fur rugs, books, lounges and chairs.

After her parents, who had never approved of Howard, succeeded in breaking up their daughter's marriage, Lillie stayed more and more at Larkmead, which she called her vineyard estate because of the many birds around it.

"Independent, unconventional, frank and somewhat barbaric," according to her biographer, Lillie finally left her picturesque Napa Valley home in 1887 and never returned to Larkmead. She rented out the estate and went to live in Europe.

She returned to the City, where she died July 22, 1929. Lonely was sold to Mr. and Mrs. Ren Bothe and the lower part of the estate to others, among them the Morosoli-Salmina family. Larkmead was left to deteriorate and burn, all except the three tall palms which mark the spot where the bungalow once stood. Those trees still stand today, out in the vineyard, a short distance from the Trail near Larkmead Lane.

In Lillie's memory, $100,000 was donated to San Francisco to erect the now world-famous Coit Tower on Telegraph Hill and a monument to the firemen of her company in Washington Square.

Stevenson at Silverado

I T was late May of 1880.

Townsfolk in their Sunday best had trooped to the railway station, as was their wont, to stare at the new arrivals coming in on the train.

Few gave a second glance at the tall, gaunt young man with the longish hair and sallow complexion in the shabby velvet coat or the short thick-set woman with dark curling hair as they descended from the car—except, perhaps, to note that they made a strange couple.

The man's keen eyes took in the balding dome of the huge mountain ahead and the picturesque high-rock formations rimming the valley. Like another young man almost three decades ago, he drew in a sharp, appreciative breath. The craggy Palisades, especially when bathed in a cinnabar sunset, have a certain soul of their own which evokes the superlative in any language; and this man was a born poet. Instinctively he reached for the inevitable notebook and scribbled the first of many voluminous notes he was to make of this beautiful land and its people.

The frail newcomer was Robert Louis Stevenson, not quite thirty and just married in San Francisco to the forty-year-old former Fanny Osbourne. With them were her son, Samuel Lloyd, by a former marriage, and their dog Chuchu.

Their friends, the well-known California painter Virgil Williams and his wife Dora, had a dual purpose in inviting the Stevensons here—to spend their honeymoon at the Williamses' "small ranche" high up in the mountain country above Calistoga and also get Louis away from the "poisonous salt air and sea fogs" which seemed to be endangering his health; for he suffered from "Bluidy Jack," the consumption (as tuberculosis was then called) which plagued him most of his life.

As it turned out, the newcomers were not to take advantage of their friends' kind invitation to stay at Sugarloaf. The mountain top was too far away from fresh meat and milk and other necessities; and so the little family took a cottage at Brannan's resort, "the first inside the entrance to the grounds, near what is now a modern bathhouse," writes Mrs. Issler. This historic cottage has been moved to the side of the Calistoga pioneer museum, where it is being restored.

HOWEVER, the ten-dollars-a-week rent was too big a strain for their frugal purse. Too, Brannan's resort was "full of sulphur and boiling springs"—just the opposite of what Louis was supposed to have to regain his health.

With the help of friends and townspeople, the young couple finally located in a "rent-free" bunkhouse at the abandoned Silverado mine site, high up on the mountainside and not too far from the Williams ranch for frequent hikes across the canyon for a visit.

In the next two months, Louis was to become a familiar figure to both mountaineers and townsfolk alike, though often he was more interested in them than they in him. Louis was a good listener, and the tales they told of stage-coachmen and robbers, of miners and hunters, of pioneers and home-steaders fascinated him.

Louis roamed all over the mountain and the countryside, slowly regaining health in the dry air of Silverado and happily adjusted to his life with the loving, capable Fanny.

Stevenson was far more concerned with the comings and goings of "simple folk and places than the more sophisticated", and it was the former about whom he was to write, who were to spring to life in the pages of "The Silverado Squatters," the adventure story which eventually evolved from the many notes he meticulously kept in his journal.

Louis made friends in Calistoga, and he included many in his book: "Petrified Charlie" Evans, who one day discovered petrified trees while clearing off his pastureland out on the Santa Rosa road; the varied characters who either lived near the Lawley Toll House Inn or came and went on the stages; Jacob Schram, the German winemaker, or the Scot McEachran, both of whom lived up a tree-shaded glen below town and were more than pleased to share their wine cellars with their appreciative friend; Jacob and Frederick Beringer in their new (1876) Los Hermanos winery, which Stevenson described in "Napa Wine"; Charlie Foss, the dare-devil stagecoachman, with whom Louis was to have his first experience with the telephone — Stevenson at "Cheeseborough's" Magnolia Hotel and Foss "several miles off among desolate hills"; and, of course, the friendly townsfolk and merchants along "High Street," as Louis called Lincoln Avenue.

"All the life and most of the houses," he was to write, "are concentrated upon that street between the railway station and the road (Main Street) which runs perpendicular to both."

The L. M. Corwin census in 1880 counted 1,259 persons, "including thirty-four Chinamen," living in Calistoga and its surrounding districts and the following businesses: one bakery, three livery stables, two blacksmiths, one Chinese laundry, two shoe stores, three general stores, one furniture store, one carpenter's shop, one confectionery, one tailor's, two hardware shops, two meat markets, one barber, two hotels, one saddlery, two milliners, one jeweler, one drug store, one carriage shop, one paint store, three doctors, one real-estate agency, one newspaper, five saloons, one Wells Fargo agency and SP depot, one stage line to Lake County... Not too much different from today.

And Louis probably knew most of them by name, despite the fact that the young author spent only the first week wandering about town, prior to moving to the mountain.

After every excursion, Stevenson would return to his "palace" among the trees and boulders to write down in the journal he was painstakingly keeping the day's happenings and the comings and goings of the folk he'd met and talked with. It's just possible that Louis learned far more of Calistoga and its history and geography and people in his short stay here than most of us do in a lifetime.

Curiously, neither the editor of The St. Helena *Star* nor *The Calistogian* seemed to feel that Stevenson had news value, Mrs. Issler writes. In fact, the press thought Joe Strong, the San Francisco artist and husband of Fanny's daughter Isobel, was more newsworthy! For example, in the July 21, 1880, *Calistogian*, appeared a story about Strong's "spending some time this summer in the upper Napa Valley and about Mount Saint Helena ... in the vicinity of the Toll House ... making sketches." Nary a word about Stevenson.

Joe's sketches of Louis and Fanny, showing them inside their "palace," Louis writing in his journal in an upper bunk and Fanny sewing nearby, is famous.

MIDWAY of that summer came what Louis called an "interregnum": Fanny and "young Sam" fell ill with diphtheria, and the family had to take lodging in town, in a small cabin built by pioneer Henry Fowler, on Lincoln Avenue near "the crick." (I. C. Adams, Fowler's grandson, tells us that this cabin was later moved down to east Washington Street and added to the home of San Francisco mortician G. Iaccheri, who was building a resort nearby. That house is now the home of Louis Vermeil, Iaccheri's grandson.)

When everyone was sufficiently recovered, the Stevensons returned to the mountain but not to remain much longer at Silverado. Louis, by now much better and anxious for his parents to meet his new family, was ready to return home to Scotland.

The years that followed were spent in wandering and writing, always in search of improved health for Louis. December 7, 1889, the Stevensons finally arrived at Samoa in the South Seas. Louis was to die there in 1894.

Unlike Brannan, whose later life was spent in comparative obscurity, Stevenson grew in fame and fortune with the years. He wrote some of the most popular poems, essays and fiction of his time and is one of the few writers to become popular with young and old alike.

Robert Louis Stevenson

The original of the above etching was made by H. Coit in 1909 after a famous photograph taken by Lloyd Osbourne. Several other artists have also made sketches from this picture.

Stevenson's epitaph, written by him, is one of the world's most famous and best loved. The second verse, by the way, is not very well known, having been edited out by Louis' friend and literary adviser, Sidney Colvin. This was a common practice in the publishing field for many years, unfortunately. A classic example of this highhanded way of doing things occurred in the first printing of Dean Swift's "Gulliver's Travels" (1726).

The text was so altered by Swift's publisher, Benjamin Motte, so as not to offend unduly the political powers of Swift's day, that the writer complained in dismay that his fable had been so "basely mangled and abused and added to and blotted out by the printer" as to lose much of its meaning. The omission has since been corrected; but one can't but wonder how many literary gems have been altered or even lost to us through this practice.

Here is "Requiem" as originally written by Stevenson:

"Under the wide and starry sky
Dig the grave and let me lie.
Glad did I live and gladly die,
    And I laid me down with a will.

Here may the winds about me blow;
Here the clouds may come and go;
Here shall be rest for evermo,
    And the heart for aye shall be still.

This be the verse you grave for me:
Here he lies where he longed to be;
Home is the sailor, home from sea,
    And the hunter home from the hill."

"Home from sea" is the line Louis wrote, as can be seen from the facsimile on exhibit, in Stevenson's own handwriting, at the Silverado Museum.

It is often quoted as "Home from the sea", even on the Scot's mountain tomb in Samoa. Writing did not come easily to Stevenson; and it was his custom to "work over passages" until each word and phrase was just right. However, experts believe that the addition may have been Colvin's.

The story Louis "roughed in" at Silverado was published the first time in serial form in the Century magazine in 1883. It later came out in book form with a dedication to his long-time friends, Virgil and Dora Norton Williams, and is in three sections.

The first essay, "The Silverado Squatters," tells how the Stevensons came from San Francisco to Calistoga.

In the second, titled "In the Valley," are four famous vignettes: "Calistoga, The Petrified Forest, Napa Wine," and "The Scot Abroad."

The third is the story of life on "our mountain," titled "With the Children of Israel," and includes "To Introduce Mr. Kelmar" (actually Morris Friedberg, Lincoln Avenue merchant), "First Impressions of Silverado, The Return, The Act of Squatting, The Hunter's Family, The Sea Fogs, The Toll House, A Starry Drive, Episodes in the Story of a Mine," and "Toils and Pleasures."

100   The magazine series included several passages which

were not incorporated into book form later on, according to James D. Hart, librarian of the Bancroft Library at the University of California at Berkeley and a trustee of The Vailima Foundation, which provides funds for the Silverado Museum in St. Helena.

Professor Hart includes all the original in his "From Scotland to Silverado"—all of the Scot's previously published and unpublished works about his California experiences.

STEVENSON'S description of "our mountain" is a classic, even today.

"Calistoga was a pleasant place to dwell in ...

"And there was something satisfactory in the sight of that great mountain that enclosed us to the north: whether it stood robed in sunshine, quaking to its topmost pinnacle with the heat and brightness of the day; or whether it set itself to weaving vapours, wisp after wisp growing, trembling, fleeting, and fading in the blue.

"The tangled, woody and almost trackless foothills that enclose the valley, shutting it off from Sonoma on the west and from Yolo on the east—rough as they were in outline, dug out by winter streams, crowned by cliffy bluffs and nodding pine trees—were dwarfed into satellites by the bulk and bearing of Mount Saint Helena. She overtowered them by two-thirds of her own stature. She excelled them by the boldness of her profile. Her great summit, clear of trees and pasture, a cairn of quartz and cinnabar, rejected kinship with the dark and shaggy wilderness of lesser hilltops."

No wonder Stevenson selected this great mountain and its spectacular neighbors, which he had grown to love so well, as models for "Spy-glass Hill" and its environs when he wrote his famous adventure yarn, "Treasure Island."

IN 1969, lifetime Stevenson aficionados Norman H. Strouse and his wife Charlotte realized their dream of making their collection available and enjoyable for others by opening the Silverado Museum in the historic stone building now called The Hatchery on Railroad Avenue in St. Helena, funded through the Vailima Foundation. The latter name stems from that of the Stevensons' plantation home in Samoa.

The museum is, as has been said, a "lovely jewel." It contains almost five thousand Stevenson memorabilia, including rare first editions, original letters, and manuscripts, portraits of the author, his writing desk from Vailima, books from his library and by others about him and his works, and also original paintings relating to Stevenson and "Stevenson country," including Virgil Williams, early California painter and founder of the San Francisco School of Art, Thomas Hill and William Keith, famed Western artists.

The Silverado Museum has become a mecca for Stevenson lovers who come from all over to browse among the Scot's possessions and other memorabilia.

Curator Ellen Shaffer told me the other day (spring 1977) as she showed me around the place, that more than ten thousand visitors a year have signed the guest register since the Silverado Museum opened in 1969, a total of 62,000 as of January 18, 1977!

O N "our mountain" itself (as RLS was fond of calling it), five hundred acres have been dedicated as the Robert Louis Stevenson State Park, including the bunkhouse site and nearby mine diggings. This park was established with funds donated by Stevenson fans all over the world.

In 1975 the state set aside additional acreage, including the Palisades and Swartz Canyon. Mostly undeveloped as yet, there are now 3,203.47 acres marked for an expanded RLS State Park.

Forestry crews have carved a path up the hill from the Lake County Highway to the glen, and thousands of pilgrims have made the climb to the spot where Louis and his family once lived.

In 1911 the women's clubs of Napa County marked the bunkhouse site with a granite pedestal, topped with an open-book tablet on which is inscribed the Scot's own words:

"Doomed to know not Winter, only Spring, a being
Trod the flowery April blithely for a while,
Took his fill of music, joy of thought and seeing
Came and stayed and went, nor ever ceased to smile."

"It can be guessed," says biographer Issler, "that in some poet's Valhalla Robert Louis Stevenson has never ceased to smile."

Napa Valley women's clubs dedicated this memorial to Robert Louis Stevenson on Mount St. Helena in 1911. Among those attending were, at right, Calistoga druggist and Mrs. Charles Armstrong; in center, Agnes Safley Fisher, wife of W. F. Fisher, owner and operator of an early stage line and first supplier of water to the city of Calistoga. Couple at left unknown. — I.C. Adams photo, now in possession of Pete Molinari.

Appendix

1. *Historical Information Regarding R. P. Tucker and the White Church Property*

Within the Bothe-Napa Valley State Park is a commemorative plaque which refers to the White Memorial Church.

Mr. Reason P. Tucker (sometimes spelled Reasin) was a member of the party which came across the plains along with the ill-fated Donner Party. At Salt Lake City the train separated, due to internal quarrels; and Tucker, his wife and family and two brothers, with their families, were a part of the group who separated from the Donner group and made their way safely to Sutter's Fort.

The following spring they were still at Sutter's Fort when word came of the Donner tragedy, and Sutter appointed R. P. Tucker captain of the rescue group, who were instrumental in bringing the survivors to safety.

R. P. Tucker himself took responsibility for one of the survivors, and this young widow joined him and his family when they moved to Napa Valley, where R. P. Tucker and his brothers each bought tracts of land just south of what is now the City of Calistoga. The widow became the teacher of the first school in Napa County, near St. Helena.

The land which R. P. Tucker obtained was originally a portion of the Bale Estate. It appears that Dr. Edward T. Bale had obtained Rancho Carne Humaná in 1846 from the Mexican Governor. He married the niece of General Vallejo, who apparently had expensive tastes. In order to support an expensive wife, Dr. Bale became probably the first real estate operator in California, conveying several parcels of his Rancho to other parties for considerations.

One of the transactions was to a Mr. (Elias) Barnett, with whom a contract was made to do certain work at the Bale Mill.

Mr. Barnett never signed the contract but did do the work; and for this he believed he had earned the land and thereupon sold some of it to said R. P. Tucker about 1848, and to others, including George Tucker, a brother of R. P. Tucker.

Dr. Bale died before the United States Government had confirmed his ownership of the Rancho; and his heirs, primarily the widow, Maria Ignacio de Bale, carried on the request for Federal confirmation through the courts.

The patent of said rancho was confirmed in the heirs of Dr. Bale by United States Court Case #14504 in 1855, and a survey was ordered to determine its extent. The completed survey indicated that Rancho Carne Humana was materially smaller than was the belief of Dr. Bale, and in 1860 Maria Bale sued the United States government in District Court in San Francisco, Case #166, to demand a re-survey which would include all the land that was claimed. Subsequently there were several appeals in the case which became Case #47 in the appeals.

Inasmuch as some of the purchasers of land from Bale found that their land extended out of the Federal survey, three of them became intervenors in the case, requesting that the Bale lands be resurveyed to include all of their purchasers.

One of these was Ritchie after whom Ritchie Creek was named, one was R. P. Tucker and one was Sam Brannan.

In the meantime, about 1852, R. P. Tucker had quit-claimed a parcel of land to the Board of Trustees of the Methodist-Episcopal Church (being the first Methodist-Episcopal Church in Napa County), and whose first pastor was Reverend Asa White. The church building was built and a cemetery established on the property, the exact location of which was obscure at the time, as to whether it was on or off the original Bale Rancho as surveyed. The legal description bears little connection to the Rancho lines.

The final United States Court decision of the above case was against Bale as of September 4, 1879, and, as surveyed by Tracy, established the property line as dividing the church property.

Simultaneously, there were two actions in the State courts, the (sic) District Court of Napa County: It appears that another of the heirs of Bale (his daughter, who married a Mr. Louis Bruck) sued said R. P. Tucker and George Tucker with several others, in Case #662, for the land that had been sold by the above-mentioned Barnett to Tucker, claiming that the conveyance to Barnett had never been legally consummated. Whether the contract had been actually completed by reason of the work

105

having been done by Barnett was the matter at issue before the court. The Supreme Court of California held in 1872 that the claim by Barnett for the land had not been completely fulfilled by the work and therefore the contract was not an executory contract inasmuch as it left other work to be done. Under the circumstances, the court held, the lack of signature by Barnett on the contract prevented legal recognition of any effect as to meeting of minds of the contractors and therefore there was no legal contract and transfer of land was held invalidated. The verdict thereupon was given to Mrs. Bruck against Tucker.

Later, in Case #806, there was an additional parcel under identical condition, with identical court judgement for Bruck which, at this point, wiped out the holdings of R. P. Tucker and the church, inasmuch as Bruck refused, or neglected, to ratify the church ownership.

The church was abandoned but the cemetery still exists, the last burial having been in 1955, believed to be one of the descendants of R. P. Tucker. (Thelma Tamagni says that was Harry Tucker.)

The effect of these State cases was actually to expand the holdings of the heirs of Bale to include what is now the Bothe-Napa Valley State Park, among others. It is believed that Mrs. Bruck sold a portion of her property to Dr. (Charles) Hitchcock, and inheriting from Dr. Hitchcock was his daughter, Lillie Coit. Lillie Coit lived on the property for many years on a fairly elaborate country estate.

(Chapter Eleven is a fuller account of the lovely "Fire-belle Lillie", as she was known.)

When she sold the property to Mr. and Mrs. (Ren) Bothe, the money obtained was a part of the outlay used to build the famous Coit Tower in San Francisco.

Our records show that the State obtained the property from Mr. and Mrs. Bothe.

There is in Napa County record of a Case #1473 (Bruck vs. Hitchcock), the issue of which was water rights in Ritchie Creek. Judgement was given for Hitchcock, which confirms that water rights are now vested in the State.

As an incidental sidelight on this history, there is evidence to indicate that the school teacher who was rescued by R. P. Tucker had him as one of her pupils, inasmuch as his signature in 1852 was an "X", which had to be witnessed, but his later entry in court action dated 1864 bore a very legible "R.P. Tucker" as a signature.

The grandson of R. P. Tucker, named W. D. Tucker, still lives in Calistoga.* It is believed that he lives on the land which was a part of the property of George Tucker, brother of Reason P. Tucker, who obtained land, some of which was outside of the Bale Rancho, and remained after the lawsuits.

After the loss by court action, R. P. Tucker moved to Santa Barbara, where he set up another estate, a portion of which became Tucker Grove, a County Park donated by him to the County of Santa Barbara, which, it is believed, still exists. It would be interesting to find out if the County of Santa Barbara is aware of the history of this pioneer.

R. D. ADAMS, Land Agent

*Since deceased.

2. *The Deed to Franz Valley, 1857*

Franz Valley, which lies to the west of Calistoga, "between the valleys of Santa Rosa and Napa," according to the deed of sale to Capt. F. W. Franz in 1857, was once part of Rancho Mallacomes o Muristul y Plan de Aguas Calientes.

The late George Kettlewell, a descendant of early Franz Valley settlers, brought a copy of the deed to *The Calistogan* office one day in 1957. It reads as follows:

"THIS INDENTURE, Made this thirty-first day of January, A. D., One thousand eight hundred and fifty-seven, BETWEEN Calvin H. Blair, Thomas N. Blair, and Phineas H. Woods of Sonoma County, California, of the first part, and Frederick W. Franz of the same place of the second part, WITNESSETH, That the said parties of the first part, for and in consideration of the sum of one thousand Dollars, lawful money of the United States of America, to them in hand paid, the receipt whereof is hereby acknowledged, have granted, bargained, sold, remised, conveyed, and quit-claimed, and by these presents do grant, bargain, sell, remise, convey and quit-claim unto the said party of the second part, and to his heirs and assigns forever all the right, title and interest of the said parties of the first part of, in and to the following tract of land situated in the head waters of the creek known as Frank Bedwell's creek between the valleys of Santa Rosa and Napa in the said state and being a part of the *107* tract of land known as the J. Berryessa Rancho, and being the same tract of land heretofore occupied and improved by William Elliott and called the old Elliott place, and purchased by the said Elliott from the same Berryessa.

CALVIN H. BLAIR
THOMAS N. BLAIR
PHINEAS H. WOODS

Witness,

WILLIAM ROSS
JACKSON TEMPLE

The many stone bridges which cross streambeds throughout the county are admired world-wide as an engineering feat which has not been duplicated, according to Walt Tamagni, former road commissioner. Built around the turn of the century, some replaced crossings constructed earlier with Chinese labor.

The longest had five characteristic arches and once spanned Putah Creek in Berryessa Valley. It is now under 120 feet of water in Lake Berryessa.

Index

KAY ARCHULETA

About The Author —

Kay Archuleta has lived most of her life in the Napa Valley. She was born in Tombstone, Arizona, the eldest of eight children, and grew up in San Francisco, where she was educated in parochial schools.

Following graduation from the University of California at Berkeley, she taught school several years and also served as an accompanist and church organist.

In 1956 she joined the staff of *The Weekly Calistogan*, where she became interested in the early history of Calistoga. Out of this interest and much research has come *The Brannan Saga*.

Kay lives with her husband, a native of the Napa Valley, in "old-town" Calistoga near Pioneer Park. They are the parents of two married children, Terri, who is a high-school librarian, and Bill, a prototype machinist. Kay's hobby is painting—watercolor.

About The Illustrator —

Joe Seney is a graduate of the Maryland Institute of Art. Since 1958 he has been a free lance artist in Baltimore, Reno and Santa Clara doing advertising design, book design and illustrations. In 1974 he moved to Sonoma County and is now doing book design, illustrations, drawings and paintings for exhibition.